TEXAS AND THE MEXICAN WAR

EXTRA-ILLUSTRATED EDITION

∵

VOLUME 24
THE CHRONICLES
OF AMERICA SERIES
ALLEN JOHNSON
EDITOR

GERHARD R. LOMER
CHARLES W. JEFFERYS
ASSISTANT EDITORS

GRAVURE _ ANDERSEN _ LAMB , N.Y.

TEXAS AND
THE MEXICAN WAR

A CHRONICLE OF
THE WINNING OF THE SOUTHWEST
BY NATHANIEL W. STEPHENSON

NEW HAVEN: YALE UNIVERSITY PRESS
TORONTO: GLASGOW, BROOK & CO.
LONDON: HUMPHREY MILFORD
OXFORD UNIVERSITY PRESS
1921

To

HENRY MASSINGBIRD TUCKER

CONTENTS

ILLUSTRATIONS

TEXAS AND THE MEXICAN WAR

∴

CHAPTER I

THE EMPRESARIOS

THAT American diplomat known to his contemporaries as "the eel-like Monroe" gave Manifest Destiny a deep offense which popular memory has let slip. He bartered away, as his enemies said, our claim to the country between the Sabine and the Rio Grande. However shadowy that claim was, there were patriotic Americans in the year 1819 who wanted the country. The shadowiness of the claim was not worth mentioning, they thought. Napoleon sold us something in the Southwest and surely we, with Manifest Destiny on our side, were the best judges of what old Louisiana included. Monroe took a narrower view; and when he acquired Florida from Spain and rounded out the eastern coast line, but stopped

1

at the Sabine on the west, there was wrath in many American hearts, and some bold Americans were ready to stake their heads for the rectification of their government's error.

One of these was James Long, who led a filibustering expedition across the Mexican line in 1819. Long's exploit was the outcome of a public meeting of the citizens of Natchez, inspired by indignation over Monroe's policy. The little army of adventurers who followed Long and captured the Mexican frontier town of Nacogdoches was strangely composed and acted from a variety of motives. A noted Mexican refugee, Bernardo Gutiérrez de Lara, was associated with Long in setting up a ready-made government on the American model to preside over the new "Republic of Texas" which the invaders proclaimed at Nacogdoches. This Gutiérrez had been involved in earlier attempts to overthrow the kingdom of New Spain. Doubtless to some of Long's followers the invasion was but a detail in the revolution against Spain of which they dreamed in their vision of a new and greater Mexico. Thus, it may be, starts a delusion which we shall find all through Texan history — the delusion that a genuine republican inspiration was struggling in Mexico with reactionary monarchism.

Long's republic was short-lived. During its few months, its founder revealed that deadly serious naïveté which appeared so often in Americans of that time. Looking about for an ally, Long bethought himself of the last great pirate of American waters, Jean Lafitte, who flew the Jolly Roger over Galveston Island. Lafitte had a pirate town there, and for a while was a sovereign over the freebooters of the sea. To him Long appealed. It was while Long was absent negotiating with Lafitte that the soldiers of New Spain fell upon Nacogdoches, abolished the infant republic, and drove its survivors, whether American adventurers or Mexican dreamers, helter-skelter across the border.

After such an invasion one would expect the jealous and sensitive Spaniards to be intolerant of everything American. Yet the excitement of Long's adventure had hardly subsided when Moses Austin, a Connecticut Yankee, was granted permission to establish a colony of Americans inside the borders of New Spain. Why did the royal authorities thus contradict the logic of events? Their archives have not yet disclosed the answer. Guesses have been made, some of which must be considered. Did the Viceroy of New Spain think there was a population in our Southern States, royalist and Catholic, averse to becoming Americans and willing to be lured back into the monarchical fold? Did he feel that monarchical reënforcements were needed in Mexico as a bulwark against revolution? Or was there no deeper motive behind his action than mere favoritism? Was it, in the blunt modern phrase, only a case of "pull"? The fact that Austin had a powerful friend at court, a certain Baron de Bastrop, favors this unromantic suggestion. The riddle is still unread. But one fact is clear and full of significance: Mexico evidently had no intention of fostering an alien civilization; she prescribed methods of government for the newcomers and laid upon all the obligation to be, or to become, members of the national church.

Though Moses Austin — citizen of Connecticut, wanderer, pioneer, subject of Spain in old Louisiana, citizen of the United States again after 1803, and promoter of many ventures — obtained the grant from New Spain, his death intervened soon after; and it was his son, Stephen F. Austin, who was the real founder of Anglo-American Texas. It was he who planted the first American settlement, San Felipe de Austin, in December, 1821. Meanwhile the revolution had begun which was to result in the independence of Mexico. The revolution seems to have given a new turn to the dealings of Stephen Austin with the authorities of New Spain. In the spring of 1822, Stephen Austin, while busy with his scheme of colonization, was commanded to proceed to Mexico City to negotiate direct with the Congress of independent Mexico. At the capital, Austin met other Americans seeking, like himself, concessions from the Mexican Government. Chief among them stood that shifty General Wilkinson who had drawn Spanish pay while a great official of the United States, who had left his country for his country's good, and who was now on a hazard of new fortunes beyond the Spanish line. There, too, was Hayden Edwards, destined to become the enemy of Austin and to play a strange rôle in the history of Texas, perhaps even a deeply significant one. Other adventurers surrounded these conspicuous figures. All were clamoring for grants from the new government. Among the Mexican revolutionists there was eager discussion of many things, ranging from the practicality of the schemes of the adventurers to such high subjects as the republican ideal and the merits and demerits of slavery. In the midst of this turmoil of conflicting interests Austin found no one in a hurry to translate his informal agreement with the old authorities into a formal agreement with the new.

While Austin waited at the capital a second revolution changed the new republic into an empire, and General Itúrbide became the Emperor Agustin I. But Itúrbide's government set the example for so many later governments of Mexico by quickly collapsing. A second Mexican republic was set up and in 1824 a federal constitution was adopted. The old Spanish provinces were formed into states one of which included the three former provinces, Texas, Nuevo León, and Coahuila. Though Nuevo León was soon detached, the other two remained one state until Texas ceased to be a part of Mexico.[1]

One of the last acts of the reign of Itúrbide was a decree granting Austin the right to form a colony of Americans in Texas and prescribing the main lines upon which the new community was to be constructed (February 18, 1823). What is known

---

[1] See the accompanying map. The state was divided into three districts, those of Bexar, Monclova, and Saltillo. The district of Bexar had the boundaries of the old royal province of Texas. When the new state of Coahuila-Texas began, its legislature contained eleven members, of which only two were allotted to the district of Bexar.

as the Imperial Colonization Law of 1823 had been passed a few weeks before. The provisions of the law and of the decree, so far as Austin was affected, were confirmed by the Congress of the republic when Itúrbide fell.

The imperial decree carrying out the provisions of the colonization law instructed the Governor of Texas to apportion land either directly among immigrant families or indirectly through *empresarios* who should agree to bring in not less than two hundred families. Each family was to adopt as its occupation either farming or grazing. Each farming family was to have 177 acres of land; each grazing family, 4428 acres. Austin, if he brought in as many as two hundred families, was to have 354 acres of farm land and about 66,000 acres of grazing land. All his immigrants were to "prove that they are Roman Apostolic Catholics, and of steady habits," and he was to found a town, organize his colonists as a militia, preserve order, and administer justice.

The land granted to Austin, which was rapidly taken up by his colonists, lay between the San Jacinto and Lavaca rivers, on the Gulf side of the one Texan highway, the trail from Nacogdoches to San Antonio. His capital was the new town, on the Brazos River, San Felipe de Austin.   For the government of his colony Austin himself drew up a code of laws almost paternal in temper, including a prohibition of gambling and imprisonment for debt.

In 1824 the Mexican Republic enacted a colonization law similar to the former imperial law, but leaving many details to the local authorities.   Between the lines of this law we glimpse a shadow of uneasiness.   Mexico reserved the right to "take such precautionary measures as it may deem expedient for the security of the confederation, in respect to the foreigners who may settle within it."   The question whether slavery should be continued in Mexico had already been raised.   The national colonization laws were silent on the subject.   A state colonization law of Coahuila and Texas, enacted in 1825, provided merely that, "in regard to the introduction of slaves, the new settlers shall subject themselves to the laws that are now, and shall be hereafter established on the subject."   The newcomers did not hesitate to bring with them their slaves.

The Texas that was the consequence of these laws was a mosaic.   Theoretically a Spanish country, it was dotted with colonies of foreigners.   Each colony formed a tiny state embedded in the recognized state of Coahuila and Texas. To establish the colony an empresario or contractor was empowered to bring in a stated number of families and to allot to each family a specified amount of land within a definite area. This group was given local rights similar to those of other Mexican communities, with an *ayuntamiento* or local council, elected by the people.

The purpose of the Mexican republicans in permitting the creation of these colonies of foreigners has not been explained any more than have the purposes of the royalists who began the work by encouraging Austin. The Spanish tradition ran counter to such a policy. If circumstantial evidence counts for anything, the Mexican authorities had some vision of a new régime which Americans do not yet understand. One thing is certain: they had no intention to leave the colonies permanently separate from the rest of the population. Only the Spanish language was to be used in public transactions. A colonist who married a Mexican was allowed more land than one who did not. All the laws repeated or implied the provision of the original grant to Austin, which laid down as "the first and principal requisite for colonists that of being Catholics or agreeing to become so."

It was under these laws that Americans crowded into Texas from 1822 forward. Here appears one of the shadowy places in Texan history. How exact was their knowledge of the situation? What was their conception of the obligations the laws required them to assume? Did all of them, did even most of them, know they were supposed to join the Church of Rome? The old style historian, with his eyes fixed on slavery and on constitutional issues, ignored these questions and the new historians have not yet answered them. Why Mexico, after hedging these aliens about with such stringent regulations, left them for a number of years to their own devices, letting them come as they chose without enforcing the restrictive laws — all this still awaits research.

Whatever motive may have guided them, thousands of Americans felt an irresistible desire to pitch their tents in the sunset. From every section, from every class, pilgrims were drawn to Texas, the very seat of fortune in the American mind during the twenties. Its noble woods, its great prairies, the land that could be had for next to nothing — these were potent magnets. Furthermore, it was the land of romance, of mystery. It was the borderland of the strange Spanish world.

To the adventurous soul, it called in the deep murmur of the forest, in the wind across the trackless prairie — "I am the Unknown!" To the dreamer of democracy, it whispered grimly of possible revolution, of the last death-struggle between the people and the kings. The upholder of slavery saw in Texas a possible new lease of life for his peculiar institution. The abolitionist saw in it the possibility of a new free State. The patriot of sectionalism, if a Southerner, dreamed of expanding his section by the addition of the Southwest. Another sort of patriot, believing ardently that Texas had been filched from his country by diplomacy, turned westward, resolute to recover it, whether by fair means or by foul. Young and old, rich and poor, wise and foolish, a great host of Americans poured into the colonies of Texas in the high days of the twenties.

Out of the crowd of empresarios, the leaders of this migration, two men stand forth as makers of history. These were the younger Austin and Hayden Edwards. The character and adventures of Stephen Austin will one day inform a biography of singular interest. For the present he is eclipsed, or nearly so, by that bolder, more bulky personality which dominates the later history of Texas, Sam

Houston. But Austin will eventually come to his own. A resolute, but also a patient man, he may not have equaled Houston in driving force; but in steadfastness he was second to none. From the start to the finish he was true to his conception of his obligation to Mexico. For this we have his own words, and he was a man of principle whose words must be accepted. But just what his conception was it is not easy to say. Though he made a hard and fast religious agreement with Mexico, he did not live up to it, and there seems little doubt that he felt free to disregard it. Strangely enough, his biographers, apparently indifferent on this point, have never troubled themselves to go in search of his own defense; their lightly sketched, half-articulate explanations leave the subject dark. That he probably considered the religious agreement a conventional survival of the old order which was, as he thought, perishing in Mexico and which he believed would vanish presently along with last night's darkness — that he interpreted as evidence of this, Mexico's utter failure to enforce the agreement — is at present a plausible hypothesis. What is definite, what sets him off in sharp contrast with Edwards, is his resolute attempt to become part of Mexico. Neither Austin nor Mexico understood

the other. Mexico did not realize that it was under-
mining itself by introducing the Americans. Austin saw no reason why the two races with their
differing civilizations should not occupy the same
territory, and though with the simplicity of his
period he understood himself as little as Mexico
did, he fought hard to maintain the impossible new
condition — impossible for reasons that will develop as the tale proceeds — and struck hard at
the first head reared in opposition.

Edwards, on the other hand, was among those
who looked upon the Mexicans as the real intruders
north of the Rio Grande, upon themselves as the
rightful owners of the soil, and upon the possession
of it as their chief aim in life. His previous history
is obscure. Henry Yoakum, the early historian of
Texas, calls him "a wealthy and intelligent gentleman." His enemy, Austin, accused him of having been a professional gambler at Mexico City.
He was one of the adventurers who surrounded the
sinister figure of Wilkinson during the intrigues
there in 1823. He had succeeded in getting himself
made an empresario and had fixed the site of his
colony — perhaps by design, perhaps by accident —
as close as possible to the boundary of Louisiana
and near to Nacogdoches, which had been the seat

of Long's short-lived republic.   That Edwards had Long's adventure in mind is not unlikely.

On the face of the record the revolt of Hayden Edwards and his followers against the Republic of Mexico, which followed, grew out of the question of land titles.   The region in which Edwards's colony was situated had suffered for twenty years from others besides Long.   Many of the native landowners had fled from their homes.   Nevertheless, their lands still belonged to them.   In selecting land for his colonists, Edwards was naturally required to avoid the holdings of these absentees. But he did not do so.   Was it merely because he was a rough man with a high temper?   This easy explanation is not wholly satisfactory.   In the minds of most of the Americans who went to Texas was fixed the idea that the earth belongs to him who gives it value.   Edwards and his associates looked upon themselves as the sole creators of land-value in their colony, and the return of Mexicans who had failed to hold their own was to them as the red rag that inflames the bull.   Finally, many honestly believed that the soil belonged to the United States, that all good Americans thought so, and that any one who did not was a poltroon.   Now and then in history a bold adventurer has risked his head in an attempt to commit his country to an extreme course. He puts his life on the hazard, believing his countrymen, whatever their attitude hitherto, will be so wrought upon by his daring that they will take up his battle cry and spring to arms. It will appear in a moment that Edwards conceivably was one of these great gamblers.

A decree of the Governor of the state canceled Edwards's contract and ordered him out of the country. Edwards demanded the privilege of appeal to the Federal Government. The Governor replied that he might do what he pleased hereafter, but now he must go. Edwards's first thought seems to have been that all Americans in all the colonies would stand by him. He sent posthaste to Austin for assistance, which was instantly refused. Thereupon Edwards put his head on the hazard. With a mere handful of followers he seized the town of Nacogdoches and proclaimed an independent republic which he styled Fredonia. For assistance against Mexico, he appealed to Americans everywhere and even contracted an alliance with the Cherokee Indians. He succeeded in raising an army of two hundred men. On December 21, 1826, the Republic of Fredonia, in true American style, adopted a complete constitution.

The revolt was quickly put down. Not only did the colonists fail to respond to Edwards's appeal, but Austin helped to raise a considerable force that joined the Mexicans in an attack on Nacogdoches. Edwards at that moment was seeking aid across the near border, in Louisiana. But before the end of January all was over. The former empresario was a landless man on the east side of the Sabine and his handful of followers were dispersed or prisoners.

And yet Hayden Edwards had made history.

CHAPTER II

THE Fredonian revolt was the sensation of the hour both in the United States and in Mexico. American newspapers in 1827 teemed with reports of the "Fredonian War" — the war of two hundred men against a nation — and with expressions of sympathy with the Fredonians. The American people, having in them the egoistic passion of the Lord's Anointed, saw nothing of the point of view of the Mexicans. Democracy, freedom of the individual, as Americans conceived it, was for them the supreme law. No delicate questions of legal right or of the political duty of the revolters were allowed to color the main theme. In sharpest black and white the ardent Americans of 1827 pictured their kinsmen defeated in Mexico as apostles of democracy crushed by an alien civilization.

Mexico took alarm. A startled consciousness seized the Mexican leaders that their colonizing policy had overshot the mark. In their effort to get a hardy new population they had created a power that now threatened to turn and rend them. It was the story of Frankenstein translated into terms of politics. Immediately there was proposed the simple but now dangerous course of reversing the colonization policy and prohibiting further immigration from the United States. Obregon, the Mexican Minister at Washington, reporting to his Government the widespread sympathy for Fredonia in the United States, gave as the only solution the closing of the Mexican frontier against Americans. In the Mexican Congress the Washington Government was bluntly charged with complicity in the Fredonian war. A powerful newspaper at Mexico City, *El Sol*, put the accusation into public print. The President of Mexico told the American Minister, Joel R. Poinsett, he did not believe the charge but said he hoped the President of the United States would publicly deny it.

As early as February, 1827, indeed, Obregon had interviewed Henry Clay, Secretary of State, hoping for such a denial. He wished to be reassured that he was right in thinking that the United States Government had no official connection with the

Fredonian revolt.   Clay in perfect sincerity gave him "the assurance . . . that the Government of the United States has not given the slightest countenance or encouragement to these disturbances." The Minister wrote home that he believed Clay. But he knew something of American history.   He knew that immigrants from the United States, settled in Spanish territory, had in times past stirred up revolts, and that those revolts had increased the international tension which finally led to the American occupation of the Floridas.   Whatever the Government of the United States might do or not do, the people wanted Texas, just as they had wanted Florida; their hearts were with their kinsmen beyond the Sabine; and Mexico must put herself on guard.

At this juncture the Administration at Washington made a bad blunder.   For all their imposing talents, neither John Quincy Adams at the White House nor Henry Clay in the Department of State, had the essential qualities of the diplomat.   They were both racial egoists, unable to understand an alien race.   Unfortunately the Minister at Mexico shared their limitation.   He had misunderstood the Mexican character so thoroughly that his dispatches to Clay created at Washington the false impression on which Adams and Clay now decided to act. Nearly two years earlier Poinsett had written to Clay that, in spite of intense contrary feeling, Mexico would soon find Texas such a thorny problem that she would consent to part with it. Clay apparently reasoned that all Mexico had needed was a demonstration of her difficulties in Texas, which he thought she now had. "Impressed with these views," he wrote to Poinsett, "the President has thought that the present might be an auspicious period for urging a negotiation at Mexico, to settle the boundaries between the two republics."

This proposal sounds innocent enough, but the conditions of the moment gave it a sinister meaning. Once the United States had claimed the Rio Grande as the boundary of Louisiana. The withdrawal to the river Sabine, and the acceptance of that line in the treaty of 1819 had been bitterly denounced in the United States. Thousands of Americans believed that they were entitled to "recover" the territory between the Sabine and the Rio Grande. On the other hand, when Poinsett first began sounding the Mexican Government on the subject, he found a very different idea. The Mexicans made an astonishing claim. They held that the King of Spain never had authority to alienate any part of the Spanish domain in America, that the treaty of 1819 was therefore null and not binding on Mexico; and it was even intimated that the true boundary between the two countries was the old line of the treaty of 1795 which would extend Mexico to the Mississippi. There were still other considerations. The story of Poinsett in Mexico is a strange and obscure tale. He was accused of taking part in Mexican politics. In 1827 rumors about his political improprieties were a floating scandal at Mexico City. That there was foundation for them he himself confessed in a letter to President Adams. He told of his attempt to rally and consolidate the friends of "our Republican principles" in Mexico by drawing them into a grand lodge of York Freemasons that was to rival the older Mexican foundation of Scottish Rite Freemasons. The branches of the Masonic body thus arrayed against each other became the bases of two political parties. No wonder Poinsett's most careful critic calls his course "amazingly imprudent."

In the spring of 1827 Mexico still withheld its endorsement from the treaty of 1819 and the United States had not accepted a commercial treaty negotiated by Poinsett the year before; and the bitterness over Fredonia still charged the air when President Adams, through Clay, directed Poinsett to offer Mexico in return for all the Texan country to the banks of the Rio Grande the princely sum of one million dollars. But opinion in Mexico with regard to the boundary had crystallized; to meet the United States at the Sabine and fight it out there became the accepted policy. In April the Mexican Congress resolved that it would not complete the commercial treaty unless the United States pledged itself to accept the Sabine as a boundary. In the following month Poinsett began sounding the minds of the Mexican statesmen on the subject of the Rio Grande, and was soon convinced that the project was hopeless — at least for the present — and then, he wrote Clay, he "abandoned it altogether." A premature statement, as we shall see.

So lacking in diplomatic prescience were all three of the American managers that they saw nothing suspicious in the next move made by Mexico. A Mexican commission started northward in the autumn of 1827 to examine the country along the proposed boundary. Nothing suspicious in this! Yet at that very time Poinsett wrote that the only thing to do was to accept the line of the Sabine and complete the pending commercial treaty on that understanding. Early in 1828, Mexico met Poinsett on his new ground, accepted his proposition, agreed to the revised commercial treaty and to another, destined to be known as the Treaty of Limits, fixing the boundary at the Sabine.

This action, however, did not turn the course of the Mexican boundary commissioner, Don Manuel de Mier y Terán, a learned and able man, devotedly patriotic. He continued his leisurely journey through Texas to Nacogdoches where in 1827 a small Mexican force commanded by Colonel Piedras had been stationed. This officer was often involved unpleasantly with the colonists of that region, who wanted to know why his garrison was there. It may have been this that moved the Mexican authorities to instruct Terán as follows: "Further, the Government desires that Your Excellency in passing beyond the frontiers which we actually hold, will report whether or not there is any necessity for fortifying any points along the same for the necessity of the interior, once the exact boundary is established." About the middle of the next year, having finished his "geographical investigation," Terán sent to Mexico a long and interesting description of the Texan community.

As one covers the distance from Béjar to this town [Nacogdoches], he will note that Mexican influence is proportionately diminished until on arriving at this place he will see that it is almost nothing. . . . The ratio of Mexicans to foreigners is one to ten. . . . The Mexicans of this town comprising . . . the lowest class. . . . The naturalized North Americans in the town maintain an English school, and send their children north for further education. . . . Thus I tell myself that it could not be otherwise than that from such a state of affairs should arise an antagonism between the Mexicans and the foreigners which is not the least of the smouldering fires I have discovered. Therefore, I now warn you to take timely measures. Texas could throw the whole nation into revolution. . . .

The wealthy Americans of Louisiana and other Western states are anxious to secure land in Texas for speculation but they are restrained by the laws prohibiting slavery. If these laws should be repealed — which God forbid — in a few years Texas would be a powerful state which could compete in wealth and productions with Louisiana. The repeal of these laws is a point toward which the colonists are directing their efforts. They have already succeeded in getting from the Congress of Coahuila a law very favorable to their prosperity; the state government has declared that it will recognize contracts made with servants before coming to this country, and the colonists are thus assured of ample labor which can be secured at a very low price in the United States.

Among the ideas which were taking form in the alert mind of Terán, here is one of the most important. The Texans had a great economic advantage over the rest of Mexico in their possession of slaves. And they were holding slaves in defiance of Mexican national law. Local laws also in theory had abolished slavery. The state constitution of Coahuila and Texas, adopted in 1827, emancipated all future children of slaves and forbade bringing in slaves after six months. But the influence of the Texans had brought about the other slavery law to which Terán refers. This piece of legislation was not two months old, when Terán singled it out as dangerous. Under this law, the newcomer from the United States just before crossing the border made a contract with his slaves, which the State of Coahuila would respect. Thus slaveholding settlers continued to come in. Terán saw the difference in prosperity between Texas and Mexico and fixed on the labor supply as the prime, though not the only, cause; and to destroy the supply of slave labor in Texas became henceforth one of his chief designs.

In the spring of 1829 Terán left Texas. He and

Austin had become friends. That his visit had made history, and that it was the beginning of the end of their peace, had probably not entered the minds of any of the Texans who had been the hosts of this accomplished and delightful gentleman.

The year 1829 was eventful in the history of Texas, Mexico, and the United States. In that year Spain made an attempt to reconquer Mexico — a wholly foolish endeavor that began in July and collapsed in September at Tampico, without apparent result except a great reputation for the Mexican general, Santa Anna. Second in command against the invaders was Terán. The repulse of the Spaniards left him a conspicuous figure as *commandante general* of the Eastern States of Mexico.

It was while the Spanish fiasco was in progress that a momentous interview took place at Washington. Andrew Jackson, now six months President, gave audience to an adventurer named Anthony Butler and was wholly persuaded by him. Butler had been in Texas. He was confident that all Adams had failed to do two years before could yet be done — only the price must be raised. Give him five million dollars instead of one million, and he would deliver Texas into Jackson's hands.

A critic has written of Butler that "he lacked moral character and fitness for any position of trust" and "was charged with being a speculator in Texan lands, a gambler, a drunkard, and a liar." Jackson himself finally dubbed Butler a liar; but that was after they had fallen out. In 1829 Butler convinced both Jackson and his Secretary of State, Martin Van Buren. Now followed a repetition of the diplomatic blunder of 1827. Just as Adams and Clay at precisely the wrong moment followed up the vagaries of Poinsett, so now, at an even more critical time, Jackson and Van Buren became fatuous disciples of a commercial-diplomatic soldier of fortune. To Poinsett, still at Mexico City, they addressed instructions, which Butler was to deliver, to try again to purchase Texas.

During the two years since Poinsett "abandoned" the scheme, while the gracious spy Terán was in Texas, the relations between Washington and Mexico had again become strained. A series of small filibustering expeditions, all starting either from or near New Orleans, had irritated the Mexican authorities. Within a month of the conference between Jackson and Butler, the Mexican authorities complained that recruits for the Spanish Government were being gathered at New Orleans and that there were suspicious military preparations at other places in the United States. Poinsett vigorously denied that these reports were well founded. But, the quarrel between him and the Mexican authorities had now run its venomous course to an irreconcilable issue. While Butler was on his way to Mexico, President Guerrero demanded Poinsett's recall. Jackson immediately complied and appointed Butler in his place.

Another cause of friction between the republics was the treatment of the two treaties negotiated by Poinsett. President Adams, accepting the second thought of Poinsett, had dropped the matter of the Texas purchase, and submitted his treaties to the Senate. The treaties provided that ratifications should be exchanged at Washington within four months of the close of negotiations at Mexico City, which would be May 12, 1828. The Senate promptly authorized ratification, but the Mexicans were so slow that their ratification did not reach Washington until August, after the Senate had adjourned. Negotiation could be revived only by submitting the treaties to the next session of Congress. Before then, the presidential election took place, Jackson triumphed over Adams, and the latter determined to hand over the Texan

question in all its thorniness to his successful rival.
When Jackson's strange minister, Anthony Butler,
succeeded Poinsett late in 1829, he found himself
in the same situation as his predecessor two years
before. Two treaties were hanging fire; both countries carried chips on their shoulders; the United
States, though innocent of any hostile act toward
Mexico, was scheming to profit by her distress.
At Washington there was no comprehension of the
out-at-elbows pride of the average Mexican, his
vanity, and his fierce dreaminess; nor of the existence of shrewd and experienced men of the world
such as Terán south of the Rio Grande. Meanwhile at Mexico City, President Guerrero and his
cabinet were laying a plan for the "saving of
Texas." This takes us back to Terán.

In the latter half of 1829, while Jackson and Butler were maturing their five-million dollar scheme,
Terán, the commander for the Eastern States,
made Texas the constant theme of his reports
to the Mexican War Department. A crisis was
approaching. "He who consents to, or does not
oppose the loss of Texas," wrote Terán to the
Minister of War "is an execrable traitor." To his
plan of shutting off the Texan labor supply, he
now added two other schemes: the country must

be occupied by military garrisons; and colonies of Mexicans should be formed to counterbalance the existing colonies of Americans.

At first glance Terán seems to have been defeating his own ends during these later months of 1829. By this time he was not alone in his belief that Texas could be struck hard by the enforcement of the anti-slavery laws.   On September 15, 1829, a decree of President Guerrero aimed to make effective the abolition of slavery throughout Mexico. But strangely enough this decree never went into effect in Texas.   There was instantaneous protest from the colonies.   Led by Austin, they prevailed on the Governor of Coahuila to intervene with the President.   Terán now appears in a curious rôle. While Austin and the colonists were protesting, and before it was known what Guerrero would do, Terán from his headquarters at Tampico wrote to Austin that Guerrero had authorized him to except Texas from the main provisions of the decree.   He added that it would not be necessary to publish the decree in Texas.   In December Guerrero formally confirmed Terán's promise.   What had happened behind the scenes at Mexico City?   There is a letter from Austin to Terán thanking him for his intervention.   But this would only increase the

mystery, were it not for the following sentence in a famous Mexican state paper, the *Iniciativa* of Lúcas Alaman: "Such is the independence enjoyed by the North American colonists and to such a point have the privileges accorded them borne fruit that when the decree of September 15 . . . abolishing slavery was issued . . . the commander of the frontier of that State said he could not hope to see such a decree obeyed unless it should be enforced by a larger military force than he then had." In short, the Government had been premature, for Terán's military preparations were not complete.

To make sure that the Government fully understood the situation, Terán sent early in January an extensive report describing in detail his plan for "saving Mexico," including his military and colonization plans. Meanwhile Butler had arrived. He had come through Texas, and apparently had talked along the way, for three days after Terán's report came in, *El Sol* was shouting at the United States. "A few days after the departure of Mr. Poinsett from this capitol," said that newspaper, "the American Colonel Butler arrived here commissioned, as it is said by the Government at Washington, to negotiate with ours for the cession of the province of Texas for the sum of five millions of dollars. As we are not informed that, so far, the Colonel has made any overtures on the subject, we presume that he does the . . . administration the justice to suppose it incapable of lending itself to a transaction as prejudicial and degrading to the republic as it would be disgraceful to the minister who would subscribe to it."

This outburst in *El Sol* was not the only protest. The flood gates were opened. As in 1827, so now the proposal to buy Texas roused to fever heat Mexican distrust of the United States. Here was the arch enemy at his old tricks seeking to dismember Mexico. American newspapers, it was said, were urging Jackson to seize Texas. Butler like Poinsett fell into a panic, faced about, revived the dormant treaties, and fell back upon the line of the Sabine. On those terms the two treaties were eventually accepted by Jackson, who saw, even before his agent, that he had stumbled into a hornets' nest.

The fate of Texas was thus in part decided by the indiscretion of the American president and his minister; still more by the resource and determination of Terán; lastly by the Mexican minister of foreign relations, Lúcas Alaman. Building upon Terán's report, while that enterprising official went

ANTONIO LÓPEZ DE SANTA ANNA

Wood engraving, after a photograph. In the Print Department
of the New York Public Library.

Gravure, Andersen-Lamb, Co. N.Y.

on with his military preparations, Alaman drew up his *Iniciativa*, or project, on which was based the fateful decree issued by the Mexican Congress on April 6, 1830. Though closely following Terán, Alaman had added a history-making provision of his own. In Article Eleven of the famous decree "it is prohibited that emigrants from nations bordering on this Republic shall settle in the states or territory adjacent to their own nation."

When the decree was passed, Terán was at Matamoras, where he had begun to concentrate his army several weeks before. As suave and adroit as he was resolute, he spent April and May communicating with prominent Texans, especially Austin, in an effort to reconcile them to the decree, but without success. In the summer of 1830 Terán led his army across the Nueces River. The struggle of the two races for Texas had begun.

3

CHAPTER III

FROM the Rio Grande one great highway crossed Texas to Béxar (San Antonio), and thence ran in nearly a straight line northeastward to Nacogdoches and the frontier. Along this road in the hot days of the summer Terán's army must have marched. From the main road, along the leafy byways that did service as minor roads, little bodies of Mexican soldiers — disreputable men in the main, some of them former convicts — vanished into the forests or struck across bits of prairie to appear presently at various little towns where they established garrisons. Having distributed his men in a dozen or more cantonments, Terán fixed his headquarters at Matamoras.

During the next eighteen months these soldiers were the absorbing topic of conversation in Texas. There was no regular mail system, and news was circulated largely by mounted traders, who, singly or in caravans, moved across the landscape, in and out of the great belts of shadowy forest, through the burning glare of the open spaces, and told the little wooden towns of Texas what they had seen. And of these things the keen-eyed, hard-muscled, restless newcomers from "the United States of the North" talked together at street corners, on hot summer evenings. They discussed the insolent Mexican "invasion," their own rights, and the possibility of getting aid from their kinsmen beyond the Sabine.

Just how did these Americans reason about their own relation to Mexican law? Just how did they excuse to themselves their serene indifference to their pledge to become Catholics and justify their intrusion of American ideals into Mexican civilization? All this is obscure. But that they felt entirely justified before their own conscience is beyond the shadow of a doubt. Two things with regard to them and their frame of mind are clear. They looked on all life with that curious, boisterous jollity — that preoccupation with the moment — which has come to be labeled American humor. They held unswervingly to the idea of "the tools to him that can use them." Subsequently Austin argued the Texas cause in the United States clearly and ably, basing his abstract argument on the idea that no natural right to the soil exists — that only as man cultivates the soil does a right to it come into being.

In addition to the social philosophy of the Texans — which was the American political philosophy of that day — the sense of humor of these people must never be forgotten. It was a very limited form of humor, to be sure, but very real. It informs one of the most interesting of the Texan documents, the *Reminiscences* of a certain Henry Smith, whom we shall meet presently as one of the chief movers in the secession from Mexico. Never was this peculiar humor displayed more fully than in a story told in the recollections of the family of Adolphus Sterne, one of the Fredonians captured by the Mexicans in January, 1827, who spent some time in prison.

He . . . wore loose boots which he could easily draw off and on his feet, and his chain was locked about them. One night, his guards locked the door of his room, and went to a fandango. Left alone he drew the boot off his chained leg, and the chain with it. Then he raised a sash, went out through a window, proceeded to his store, dressed himself properly, and made his way also to the fandango. There he found his guards who were much startled by his arrival; but he and they promised not to inform against each other, and all were easy. One of his friends in surprise said to him:

"Why, Sterne, how came you here?"

"I walked," was the reply.

"But why are you here?"

"To dance, of course."

And dance he did. In good time, he returned to his store, resumed his prison garb, went back to his prison, reëntered it through the window, and drew on his boot, and the chain with it. When his guards returned, they found him as they had left him.

If we remember the unswerving belief of the Americans in Texas, that the earth belongs to him whose labor gives it value, and their humorous attitude towards things Spanish or Mexican, and add to these a certain rough cleanness of heart and a contempt for intrigue, we can at least partly understand their view of the decadent Latins of Mexico.

The Texans being what they were, the Mexicans and their convict soldiers being what they were, the remarkable aspect of the matter is that more than eighteen months went by before a serious clash occurred. Bickerings there were, of course, without number. During the latter part of 1830 and the whole of 1831 the colonists and these men whom they regarded as unscrupulous invaders became steadily more and more exasperated. The chief bone of contention was a question of customs duties. By the laws of 1823 the colonists were exempted from duties for a period of seven years. Terán's invasion came just at the end of this period. The Mexican tariff that now became binding on the colonists prohibited the importation of a long list of ordinary necessities of an agricultural community; and the nearest Mexican trading centers were separated from the Texan colonies by hundreds of miles of what was then considered desert, where there was constant danger of Indian raids. The difficulties of such trading were great as compared with the easy trade by sea from New Orleans. The colonists received little satisfaction from a concession of the Government allowing free importation of certain necessities for a period of two years, but only through two ports, one of which was Anáhuac at the head of Galveston Bay.

Terán made a great blunder by placing in command at Anáhuac John Davis Bradburn, a soldier of fortune from the United States. Even if Bradburn's harshness has been exaggerated in Texan tradition, there seems no doubt that he was a hard, fierce man, quite unsuited to the complex situation over which he was expected to play the

Olympian. Chief in a series of clashes between Bradburn and the Texans was a direct defiance of his authority as collector of customs. This episode took place at Brazoria. By a somewhat informal arrangement, Terán had permitted the landing of goods at the mouth of the Brazos River under the oversight of Bradburn. The arrangement was not satisfactory, and the Government soon accused the shippers of extensive smuggling, especially of arms and ammunition. When the crews of three schooners set the customs officers at defiance in December, 1831, the people of the neighborhood sided with the sailors and joined in a demonstration very like a riot. The sailors made their escape; but Terán put them under ban, by announcing that if any of them returned to Mexico they would be seized and tried forthwith. Nevertheless one of the schooners, the *Sabine*, came back the next month and, in defiance of the authorities, delivered two cannon to the people of Brazoria. This time there was a real riot which so terrified the customs officers that they fled to the woods and left Brazoria to its own devices.

Meanwhile at Anáhuac things had gone from bad to worse. The quarrel between Bradburn and his subjects has become so entangled with legend that it is now difficult to separate fact from tradition. But this much, at least, stands forth grimly definite; in May, 1832, Bradburn arrested several prominent colonists on the ground that they were obstructing his rule. This action was the signal for a revolt. Bradburn found himself suddenly surrounded in his fort at Anáhuac by a force of enraged enemies, more numerous than his garrison. He had the advantage, however, of being sheltered by the fort, and the early skirmishing was rather in his favor. Then the colonists, bethinking themselves of the cannon at Brazoria, sent off for the two pieces and sat down to besiege Bradburn.

During these same days, destiny was at work in Mexico. That Santa Anna who had been Terán's commanding officer against the Spaniards was now expanded to a great figure. He and Terán, in the three years since their close association at Tampico, had drifted in opposite directions. Santa Anna had gone the way of all flesh in Mexico and had started a revolution against the rule of Bustamante who in his time had overthrown Guerrero. Terán, relatively a conservative, sympathized with the existing Government, and was being supported in Texas by that Government. Santa Anna, a theatrical statesman with a shifty conscience, had struck the attitude of liberalism and accused the Government of tyranny. His headquarters were at Vera Cruz, where lately government forces had besieged him, but on May 13, 1832, they were repulsed. This reverse proved to be the beginning of the end for Bustamante. Simultaneously Terán, defending the old Government in the north, also suffered a defeat. He had marched upon Tampico, where the local commander had declared for Santa Anna, and had been repulsed. Thereafter, the "liberals" advanced in power with giant strides.

Though Terán was watching this great revolt in the south and was despairing of his country, he found time to order Colonel Piedras to go to Anáhuac from his own garrison town of Nacogdoches and "pacify the disturbances." That was toward the end of May. June was almost gone before Piedras started. The Texans — still without the cannon of Brazoria — were waiting for him. They captured him, made him promise to have all prisoners in the hands of Bradburn released, and sent him on his way. Piedras kept his word. The first week of July he spent at Anáhuac, releasing the prisoners and reorganizing the garrison, for Bradburn sullenly refused to continue in command. Piedras then posted back to his own town.

By this time Santa Anna and his party were carrying everything before them. Terán had lost heart beyond recovery. His death, at the opening of July, is accounted for by some as suicide, by others as assassination. Either is possible. Assassination has always been a respectable device in Mexican politics. The acute and farsighted Terán, however, may have seen only disaster for all his hopes in the success of Santa Anna and despaired of the future. Remembering his Latin tradition, it is easy to believe that he fell on his own sword.

While stern events were hurrying toward catastrophe farther south, the first real battle between Texans and Mexicans was fought. The grimly humorous Henry Smith was district commissioner at Brazoria. When the news came that cannon were needed at Anáhuac, he and others saw that the only way to take them there was by sea. But at the mouth of the river Brazos stood the fort of Velasco well garrisoned. If the cannon were to go to Anáhuac this fort must first be reduced. In his *Reminiscences* Smith has told how it was done. There was fierce battle. One cannot read Smith's plain, unboastful tale without a thrill or without thinking him justified when he adds that "take this battle altogether . . . the number engaged, the hurry in which they were called, totally undisciplined . . . to march up coolly and deliberately within thirty paces of a strong fortress of disciplined troops . . . really seems to savor more of reckless hardihood than of true courage."

But the need of cannon at Anáhuac had passed. The capture of Piedras had changed everything. Furthermore, the feeling in favor of Santa Anna had made its way even to Anáhuac. The insurgent colonists had declared themselves for the "liberal" movement. Perhaps that was one reason why Piedras had been in a hurry to go home. He was no lover of Santa Anna. While he was hurrying through the business and then taking himself off, another man of war was approaching Anáhuac from the opposite direction. This was Colonel Mejía, sent northward by the followers of Santa Anna to spread the "liberal" gospel at the point of the bayonet. While Smith and his associates, far up the coast, were storming Velasco, Mejía occupied Matamoras. This may have been the last straw that broke Terán's courage. A few days after Terán's death, Mejía set out by sea to pacify Texas and by mid-July had his army at the mouth of the Brazos. He brought with him no less a person than Austin, who, having been absent

from his colony attending in the legislature during
the Anáhuac troubles, was now returning home
and had joined Mejía at Matamoras. Shrewd and
cautious, Austin had, as he thought, perceived
which way the wind was blowing for Texas. His
prompt fraternizing with Mejía furnishes the key
to his policy. Still loyal to the Mexican connection, but opposed to the party of Terán, Austin
aimed to reconcile Texans to the rule of the liberals,
represented by Santa Anna. Sailing northward
with Santa Anna's general, he passed the depleted
garrison of Velasco marching southward on their
retreat from Texas. He was, as it were, the surety
for Mejía, when the enthusiastic people of Brazoria
gave them a public dinner, poured out fiery eloquence, and endorsed the "liberal" movement of
the glorious Santa Anna.

About the same time the spread of Santa-Anna-
ism infected the garrison at Anáhuac. Drawn ir-
resistibly by the lure of revolution they had only
one thought and that was to hasten southward to
the scene of commotion. Some made their way
overland. Bradburn in disguise escaped from the
country. The majority of the garrison packed
themselves into schooners and put out to sea. As
they reached the blue water beyond Galveston bar,

they were met by the flotilla of Mejía bringing his army to Anáhuac. Both parties being now on the same side, they joined forces. Away they went southward, Mejía leading, to join Santa Anna.

By this time the Texans had everywhere taken their cue from circumstance. Not yet prepared to secede, they saw in Santa Anna the less of two evils. While Mejía was at Brazoria, a conference of delegates from neighboring *ajuntamientos* had passed resolutions denouncing the late "militaristic" government of Terán, declaring their loyalty to Mexico, and praising Santa Anna. Now, though Mejía had gone, the work he had come to do was not quite complete. To be sure, the example of the Anáhuac garrison had proved contagious. Garrison after garrison threw their hats in the air, shouted their devotion to the new lord of misrule, abandoned their posts, and set out on hurried marches to join his army. But there was one notable exception — Piedras. With Piedras, the colonists resolved to deal. Determined to be taken seriously as followers of Santa Anna, a force of Texans, led by Colonel John W. Bullock and Colonel James W. Bowie, attacked Piedras in his garrison town of Nacogdoches   There was sharp fighting with deaths on both sides. Piedras then resigned his command, his major declared for Santa Anna, and the soldiers were permitted to follow their heart's desire southward to the field of loot and rapine and Santa Anna.

Two years were now flown since Terán with his army had entered Texas. Terán was in his grave and his army was gone. To the impressionistic Texans these years apparently had not seemed critical. Scattered over their enormous country, they did not find that their lives either on their farms or in their little towns had been seriously affected. The main area of the civil war was a long way off. General knowledge of the various local disturbances passed but slowly over the sparsely settled country, along the bridle-paths diverging from the one great road. We have some vivid pictures of life in Texas in this year of crisis. None of these, perhaps, has more curious interest today than the account in the *Reminiscences* of Henry Smith of what life was like at Brazoria in that space of deceptive quiet between the episode of the *Sabine* and the storming of Fort Velasco.

It may be well to remark here, that the colonists were presumed to be Roman Catholics, or bound to become such, as that was one of the necessary prerequisites to become a citizen—and no marriage could be consummated

by law without the presence and permission of a Priest
and none as yet had thought proper to reside amongst
us, and as necessity is the mother of invention, the
system of provisional marriages by bonding was introduced, requiring the judicial officers who were by
law Notary Publics, to take the acknowledgment of
the parties to a bond conditional on a sufficient penalty
to be married by a Roman Catholic priest as soon as an
opportunity might offer. . . .

The Government having determined to put the
colonists to every possible test, about this time, sent
all the way from the City of Mexico, a Priest to reside
among us and administer to our necessities. . . . His
sage appearance and seemingly good manners caused
him to be kindly received by the colonists as a kind of
necessary evil they could not well avoid. Every cour-
tesy and attention was paid to him and for a time he
and his parishioners got on very well together. He
never troubled them with church services, but con-
fined his duties to baptism and marriage ceremonies.
. . . He immediately issued his edict forbidding provisional marriages. . . . Immediately after his arrival a number of these old married people determined
to save trouble by having one grand wedding and give
the Padra an opportunity to do a whole sale business.
. . . Every preparation was made and a splendid
barbecue prepared, with all the necessary exhilerating
libations abundantly provided, so as to make it a day
of rural felicity. . . . The sight of a Roman Catholic
Priest was a rare show in Texas — a thing of which
they had long heard but never seen. . . . I was called
on to act as a kind of precurser . . . and take down
the names of the candidates for matrimony . . . and

make out a roll of the names of all the candidates for baptism. Now the test was to be made; though no religious societies were tolerated in Texas, yet prejudices deep rooted by early education rose up in strong opposition, and with many the idea of being baptised by a Roman Catholic Priest carried with it an everlasting stigma and disgrace. . . . I had never been baptised myself and as such was a willing candidate because necessity required it . . . but . . . I only succeeded in procuring a list of about forty out of a company of two hundred. . . . I reported my list and told the Padra that I had probably enrolled as many as he could conveniently get through with that evening. . . . I did not wish to let him know that any persisted in refusing. . . . I was requested to muster my forces. Immediately issued orders for a general parade. . . . They were marched up in solid column and formed in hollow square around the Priest's table. . . .

This curious bit of historical humor must not, however, color one's entire impression of Texas in 1832. Back of the volatile Texan amiability, things were brewing. Sam Houston, whose amazing Odyssey had now included Texas, wrote to Jackson, in 1832, that the country was ripe for appropriation by the United States. At Mexico City there was a renewal of the old suspicion of American intentions. Butler, with his infallible sense for the wrong moment, had resumed the discussion of a possible American purchase. It was firmly declined. And when he made a journey to Texas in the spring of 1832, watchful Mexicans drew their own inferences. Unfortunately, the troubles at Anáhuac culminated just as Butler was returning to Mexico. One high official in Mexico wrote to another that this coincidence revealed a general plan to annex Texas to the United States and that the discontent then active in the State of South Carolina had some relation with the revolutionary movement in Texas.

That the Nullificationists had any direct connection with the Texan revolt or that Jackson was even remotely at the back of it is now regarded as pure myth. But doubtless this belief was accepted as fact at Mexico in the autumn of 1832 and it is very probable that Mexicans saw what now happened in Texas distorted by misapprehension. But the Texans, unaware of this fixed illusion in the Mexican mind — due largely to the provincialism of the Government at Washington — thought their own conduct in the autumn of 1832 and the spring of 1833 above suspicion. By this time a general Texan sentiment had been crystallized. It was expressed in two conventions, both representative of the whole body of Anglo-Americans — as they called themselves — held in October, 1832, and in April, 1833. April opened the reign — so we may call it — of Santa Anna as President of Mexico, for his party had now prevailed throughout most of the Mexican States and was in possession of the capitol. To him and to the Mexican Congress the Texans appealed for reform of the customs laws, for the rescinding of Article Eleven of the decree of April 6, 1830, prohibiting emigration from the United States, and for the organization of their region as a separate State. The second convention went so far as to draw up a proposed Texas constitution, a copy virtually of an American State constitution, setting up the English common law as the law of the land. To present these appeals to Santa Anna, Austin, as representative of the people of Texas, set out for Mexico City and arrived there in July, 1833.

Until this time Austin had not wavered in his fidelity to Mexico. He seems also to have believed the professions of Santa Anna. Seeing the situation from the Texan angle, without realizing how events at Washington had affected Mexico, he entered the capital confident that the so-called "liberals" would be prompt to acknowledge the "Anglo-Americans" as their allies and would make haste to give them a state of their own. For even then Austin was determined to have a Texan commonwealth separate from Coahuila. "If our application is refused," he wrote home a few days after his arrival, "I shall be in favor of organizing *without it* — I see no other way of saving the country from total anarchy and ruin — I am totally done with conciliatory measures, and for the future shall be uncompromising as [to] Texas."

Austin was to be bitterly disappointed. More than two years were to pass before he again set foot in Texas. Of that time the first six months were spent in negotiations resulting in a suave promise from Santa Anna that all the Texan demands would be granted except the separation from Coahuila and this last would be granted at the earliest possible moment. Still trustful of Mexico, Austin started back. But on the way he was arrested, brought back to Mexico, and thrown into prison.

The cause of Austin's arrest needs explanation. In the autumn of 1833, before Santa Anna took up the note of conciliation, Austin, in a gloomy mood over his negotiation, had written a letter (October 2, 1833) to the authorities of the town of Béxar (San Antonio) "stating his belief that no reforms were to be gained from the government and urging it to take the lead in declaring Texas a separate State. He appears to have thought on the one hand that the Texans, if left to themselves, might go even further than that, and on the other that a movement begun by the Mexican population of Béxar would encounter less resistance from the government."[1] Ordinarily a cheerful and prudent man, Austin soon regained his more characteristic mood. In November, he came to terms with Santa Anna. In December he started home. His arrest took place January 3, 1834, at Saltillo. The Béxar authorities, more timid than he supposed, had been terrified by his suggestion, and had sent his letter to the central Government. We lack, as yet, the full version of the Mexican end of the story. But one cardinal detail is known. The mole-like diplomat, Anthony Butler, spent the autumn of 1833 trying to bribe his way toward a cession of Texas to the United States. His cynicism went the length of offering one official two hundred thousand dollars, and of reporting to Jackson that he might use some half million "of the sum to which you have limited me, in purchasing men, and the

[1] E. C. Barker, *Stephen F. Austin and the Independence of Texas*, Quarterly of the Texas State Historical Association, vol. XIII, p. 264.

remainder in purchasing the country." It is to Jackson's credit that this performance caused a burst of indignation at the White House, and led to Butler's recall. But Butler's shameful activities were the background against which the Mexican Government looked upon the Béxar letter.

The arrest of Austin marked the beginning of a gradual collapse of the Texan faith in Santa Anna. Though Austin, from prison, wrote a number of letters urging Texans to continue their fidelity to Mexico, a party of resistance began to form. And in May, 1834, Santa Anna gave it ample justification. All along his liberalism was a mere blind. Now he dropped the mask. He threw himself into the arms of the most reactionary party in Mexican politics, suppressed the Congress, and became dictator.

A new storm center now developed. The State Government of Coahuila plunged into the whirlpool of Mexican internal conflict. Most of its mad performances — such as a furious contention over the location of the capitol, and the formation of two parties, one standing for the town of Montclova, one for Saltillo — need not be described here. Eventually both factions accepted the supremacy of Santa Anna, whose general, Martin Perfecto de

Cos, with an army at his back, loomed high on the Texan horizon. The autumn of 1834 saw Santa Anna's influence established in the legislature of Coahuila. That same autumn appeared a pamphlet entitled *Security for Texas*, written by Henry Smith, now a confessed leader of the war party, that favored an open defiance to Mexico. But even at this eleventh hour the Mexican party among the Anglo-Americans, to whom Austin from his Mexican prison was writing conciliatory letters, opposed a revolt. Smith was answered in a publication of the Central Committee which had been established by the convention of the Anglo-Americans to keep general oversight of the political situation. Smith's time had not come. He failed to rouse a war furor. In spite of the imprisonment of Austin, in spite of the apostasy of Santa Anna, in spite of Cos and his army, the goodhumored, easygoing Texans were still content to trust to their luck and to wait for the situation to mend. One reason for this excessive optimism was a series of reforms passed by the erratic legislature of Coahuila. There was to be freedom of worship; English was to be permitted in transacting public business; a new judicial system was provided for; and new laws were enacted for the disposal of public land.

These state reforms of Coahuila, however pacific for the moment, turned out nevertheless to be just what was needed to reopen strife. By this time Santa Anna was frankly a reactionary. His plans included a strongly centralized government and the restoration of clerical influence, lately near its overthrow. The grant of freedom of worship by the legislature of Coahuila was, of course, like the proverbial red rag to the Mexican clericals. The failure of the Anglo-Americans to become genuine members of the Mexican church was doubtless well known. The reign of the good "Padra" of Smith's narrative had been short, and Smith intimates that he was forced to retire. What tales of the barbarous strangers did this priest carry back to Mexico? Here was a good cause for the most influential of Santa Anna's following to distrust the alien inhabitants of Coahuila.

A more vulgar bone of contention was afforded by the operation of the land laws. Land speculation is an obscure and apparently evil force moving in the darkness behind the politics of this time. Land companies which had been formed to buy up the claims of needy empresarios often practiced fraud. One unsavory detail of the career of Anthony Butler was his alleged connection with Texas land speculation. The Galveston Bay and Texas Land Company of New York, which bought out a number of empresarios and boldly cheated a greater number of American immigrants, is notorious. Butler's visit to Texas in 1832 was in company with the agent of this unscrupulous concern. Smith describes these speculators as unprincipled men who "ruled elections and had all appointments made to suit and be subservient to their own purposes." Into the hands of these interests Coahuila apparently saw fit to play. It was a short-sighted piece of chicanery. The Texans had a serious quarrel with the speculators and were quickly alienated by the vicious policy upon which Coahuila soon embarked. Santa Anna's Government, sufficiently distrustful of Coahuila on general grounds, took further alarm when the state began a reckless alienation of public lands. A crisis was reached in the spring of 1835, when enormous areas were virtually given away. Once more — for the last time, as it proved — Mexico briefly rehabilitated herself in Texan opinion by interfering to stop this abuse. In April the Mexican Congress suppressed the worst of the Coahuila land laws.

The next incident in this singular kaleidoscope

of events illustrates again that amazing combination of wrathfulness and good humor which was so typically Texan and so incomprehensible to Mexicans. While Mexican rule was thus recovering some measure of popularity in the spring of 1835, Captain Antonio Tenorio, a young officer under orders from General Cos, was trying to reëstablish an orderly custom house at Anáhuac. He had his troubles, for Anáhuac had not forgotten its old hatred of customs officers. Furthermore, the men of Anáhuac had a quicker sense of the ridiculous than Captain Tenorio and played practical jokes on him. A certain Mr. Briscoe, as Tenorio officially reported, "took from his house a box and went to the seashore to embark it"; Tenorio fell into the trap, for such it was, and attempted to arrest Briscoe and his friends. When they resisted, he "shot and wounded" one of the soldiers. Briscoe was simply playing a joke upon the collector, for when the box was opened it was found to contain nothing but rubbish.

Tenorio, uneasy in his post, had written in June for reënforcements. These Cos promised to send. The American love of a powwow was fully developed in Texas, and on the 22d of June a great convention, or mass meeting, was to meet at San

Felipe. The subject to be discussed was a recent action of General Cos. Not content with annulling the Coahuila land laws, he had paid off an old score by seizing Agustin Viesca, the President of Coahuila, and throwing him into prison. Upon this matter the Texans were in two minds. They did not warm to Viesca because he had been closely identified with the recent obnoxious land laws. On the other hand, were not their own liberties in danger if Cos had arrested Viesca illegally? The true American passion for constitutionality joined with the American love of debate and inspired the convocation at San Felipe. The meeting was greeted with a surprise. The day before, some impulsive gentlemen, indulging their curiosity, after the manner of Briscoe and his box of rubbish, had stopped a government courier and gone through his dispatches. They laid before the meeting the letter from Cos to Tenorio promising reënforcements.

Thereupon there was big talk in a high key at San Felipe. But in the end the prudent men of the "peace party" got control of the meeting, with the result that no action was taken. This outcome did not suit the hot-heads — especially William B. Travis, one of the men whom Bradburn had imprisoned three years before, who was resolved upon

vengeance. Travis set out with forty of like mind
to capture Tenorio. With the best grace in the
world Tenorio promptly surrendered and promised
to leave Texas with all his men. The little squall
having thus blown over, the goodhumored Texans
made a lion of Tenorio and took him and all his
men to a grand barbecue on the Fourth of July.
There, as a participant has recorded, "Captain
Tenorio walked among the people shaking hands
with the men and acting as if he was the hero of
the occasion."

The "war party" led by Smith attempted to
make capital out of the incident. Cos fatuously
played straight into their hands. Under orders
from the Mexican Minister of War, he issued a
demand for the surrender to the military of six
men — five ringleaders in the capture of Tenorio and
Don Lorenzo de Zavala, a Mexican politician and
an enemy of Santa Anna, who had recently taken
refuge in Texas. Cos sent orders to Colonel Ugartechea, now stationed at Béxar (San Antonio), to go
in search of the accused men with a force of cavalry.

Instantly the Texan blood was up. Since the
disappearance of Terán's army, Texas had been
virtually empty of soldiers, and the peace party
had succeeded in keeping the Anglo-Americans

quiet. But the orders of General Cos worked a revolution in popular sentiment. There was general approval of a scheme to hold a "consultation" of all the Texans, and the assembly was called for the 15th of October. When it was reported that Mexican soldiers were on the march, Travis wrote jubilantly, "We shall give them hell if they come here."

At this moment of crisis Austin returned to Texas. He had been a prisoner in Mexico eighteen months, and he had passed part of this time in the old dungeons of the Inquisition. Yet he came home with the hope that the situation might still be saved, war averted, and that the connection with Mexico might be made propitious. He found that the world had changed. His Texas of 1833, faithful to Mexico, had given place to a fiercely rebellious Texas, bent on revolution. The new state of things struck him with despair. The whole night following his arrival he "walked the beach, his mind oppressed with the gravity of the situation, forecasting the troubles ahead for Texas." A week later in an address which he made at Brazoria he dwelt upon the gravity of the hour and strongly approved the proposed consultation. In the middle of September he was at San Felipe, where

he was made the chairman of a Committee of
Safety. The Texans failed in an attempt to treat
with Cos, for he only repeated his demand for
the proscribed men and gave warning that Texas
must submit to any readjustment of its affairs decided upon by the central Government. The Committee of Safety thereupon issued an address to
the people and advised the immediate formation
of volunteer companies, since war was now their
"only resource."

And now Colonel Ugartechea at Béxar (San
Antonio) made a move that was fraught with destiny. The little town of Gonzales — sixty-four
miles east of Béxar and one of the southernmost of
the Anglo-American towns — had a six-pounder
brass cannon, to get which, Ugartechea sent a
corporal and four men with a cart. Andrew Pon-
ton, the alcalde of Gonzales, sent them back without the gun and with only a letter full of reasons.
Then the men of Gonzales removed the gun, took
their women and children to a place of safety, and
sent out a call for help.

It was Lexington and Concord over again. All
up and down the valleys of the Colorado and Brazos flew the hurry call for aid. In homestead after
homestead the man took down his rifle and set out,

on foot or on horseback, for Gonzales. On the 1st of October a hundred and sixty Texans assembled at Gonzales. There they learned that Don Francisco Castañeda, a lieutenant of Ugartechea, had come up with a Mexican force of eighty men when only eighteen Texans were holding the village, but hearing of the approach of reënforcements, he had retreated, without attempting to take the place.

The rescuing forces paused long enough to elect a colonel and a lieutenant colonel. Then, crossing the river, they gave chase to the Mexicans, and overtook them early the next morning. The Mexicans held a "commanding position," but after a short fight the Americans scattered them. One Mexican was killed and one Texan was wounded.

On this same day, October 1, 1835, General Cos with his main army, on the march from Matamoras, reached the town of Goliad, where he heard of the "battle" of Gonzales. The skirmish was a trifle in itself, but it marked the opening of a war of independence. The Texans had thrown down the glove; Cos accepted it. He went forward with his army to Béxar (San Antonio), where he was confronted by a motley array of Texans under the command of Austin. The two armies were within striking distance and a battle was imminent.

CHAPTER IV

TEXAS SECEDES

WHEN the Consultation began in November, the question of the hour was not whether Texas should strike for independence, nor whether the Mexican government was legitimate, but whether Texas should be governed by Mexican military authorities and military methods. Ever since Terán's show of force, pronouncements of real weight in Texas had coupled two ideas, fidelity to Mexico and determination not to be ruled by a military organization. At Gonzales, shortly before the fighting began, an agent of Santa Anna "found the people still desirous of maintaining peace with Mexico, yet equally determined to resist with energy the entrance of troops into their country." This agent obtained a statement from Ugartechea assuring the Anglo-Americans that he would not send troops against them. The delighted colonists were industriously circulating his letter when, like a bolt from the blue, the soldiers arrived demanding their cannon. The revulsion of feeling was instantaneous.

Furthermore, the Mexican Congress, reorganized in complete subservience to Santa Anna, had enacted a series of laws abolishing the federal constitution of 1824 and setting up a strongly centralized system. Finally a new constitution was drawn which abolished the existing state governments.

The three counts which in the later months of 1835 made up the Texan indictment of Mexico were: first, the destruction of the constitution of 1824; second, the use of military power to tyrannize a state; and third, duplicity of conduct. Upon this basis the Consultation drew up a *Declaration of causes for taking up arms against Mexico*. Though some phrases savored of independence, the heart of this manifesto was the statement that Texas would "continue faithful to Mexico, so long as that nation is governed by the constitution and laws that were framed for the government of the political association." The Consultation offered to combine with those Mexicans who stood by the constitution of 1824 and whose rights, like theirs, were "threatened by encroachments of military despots." A motion to secede was voted down by

DAVID CROCKETT

Engraving in the collection of the New York Historical Society.

a large majority. But it was significant of the temper of the assembly that for president of the provisional government which was now set up, Henry Smith was elected by a vote of 31 as against 22 for Austin. The organization of an army was provided for, and Sam Houston was made its commander. A council was created, with one representative from each municipality, to coöperate with the governor. The common law of England was made the law of the land. A more formal convention was called for March 1, 1836. Three commissioners, Stephen F. Austin, Branch T. Archer, and William H. Wharton, were instructed to proceed at once to the United States, there to enlist sympathy and to borrow money. Having accomplished so much, the Consultation adjourned on November 14, 1835.

On hearing that Austin had retired from its command, the army before Béxar (San Antonio) at once elected a new general. Their action, disregarding the new commander-in-chief appointed by the Consultation, typified both their temper and their organization. The volunteers who had assembled at Goliad resolved: "We claim, and can never surrender but with life, the right to elect freely our immediate commander." The several

5

brilliant skirmishes that took place in October were thoroughly decentralized. Austin had made no attempt to check the tendency. This spirit ruled the tumultuous councils before Béxar where Cos was besieged. Should he be attacked with whatever advantage the Texans now had, or should they fall back and wait for reorganization under the new régime? A council of war early in December decided to raise the siege and go into winter quarters.

Before this decision could be put into effect reports reached the camp that "the garrison [in Béxar] was in a tumult and much dissatisfied." There was immediately a call for volunteers to attack the city. The story goes that Benjamin R. Milam, a daring and picturesque personality, appeared among the men calling out, "Who will go with old Ben Milam into San Antonio?" A shout of acquiescence, and the assault had been determined upon. A rush by storming parties before dawn on December 5, 1835, established the Texans in the outer parts of the city. There followed five days of slow fighting while the Texans gnawed their way into the heart of the city. It was a strange battle, for the soldiers avoided the streets and did their firing chiefly from housetops. How the Americans burst through from house to house is thus described by a participant in the engagement: "We went through the old adobe and picket houses of the Mexicans, using battering rams made out of logs ten or twelve feet long. The stout men would take hold of the logs and swing them a while and let drive endwise, punching holes in the walls through which we passed. How the women and children would yell when we knocked the holes in the walls and went in." After five days of such fighting the army of Cos coiled itself like a gigantic worm — to use the simile of a great writer, of a much greater battle — writhed its way out of the city, and reassembled at the Alamo, a fortified mission building on the far side of San Antonio River. This was a poor position for defense, for it was commanded by Texan rifle fire and crowded with women and children. Cos opened negotiations and presently surrendered. He was permitted to withdraw his entire force to Mexico.

The next two months form a span of chaos in Texan history. Innumerable views and a jumble of resolute purposes created a Babel in the councils of the provisional government. First of all there was an irreconcilable difference between Governor Smith and the Council. Smith, possessed by the desire for independence, wanted to organize Texas for a defensive war. The Council, believing that there existed a Mexican faction that would fight for the old constitution, wanted to send an army southward to find and assist those hypothetical liberals. In consequence, both Governor and Council tried to control the army, and for the moment Houston found his command but a name.

The quarrel finally came to a head over a scheme to march southward against Matamoras, across the Rio Grande in Mexico. The army at San Antonio entirely on its own responsibility decided upon this move as a flanking blow at a Mexican army which was reported to be on the march for Texas. The San Antonio soldiers divided themselves into three groups: a few remained as a garrison; some withdrew to their homes; the rest set out for Matamoras. The expedition was led by Frank W. Johnson. With him was Dr. James Grant, a Scotch adventurer who had been one of the great beneficiaries under the obnoxious land laws of 1834. A somewhat sinister figure in the tragedy of the time is this Scotch physician. His interests were opposed both to an independent Texas and to a centralized Mexico. Perhaps he was working simply for his own advantage. How he destroyed himself and very nearly destroyed Texas remains to be seen.

While Johnson and Grant were starting on their unauthorized expedition, the Council, ignorant of what these adventurers were about, made a similar plan. A flank attack on the advancing Mexicans through Matamoras became the watchword of the Council. Though Houston protested against this move, the Council not only gave its official sanction to Johnson's expedition, when its destination became known, but even authorized one of its own against Matamoras which was to be organized and commanded by James W. Fannin. In all these arrangements Houston and the Governor were ignored. Governor Smith, rightly or wrongly, thought he saw therein the hand of those old enemies of his, the land speculators, the men who were typified by Grant. He flew into a rage and denounced the Council as a pack of wolves and traitors, whereupon the Council passed a resolution deposing him, and that was the end of relations between them.

The military situation in the latter part of February, 1836, had four points of focus. At San Antonio there was still a garrison, though Grant and Johnson had carried off most of its supplies.

Toward the south near the coast the army of Grant and Johnson occupied the town of San Patricio, for, hearing that Matamoras had been strongly reinforced they had lost heart for their venture and knew not which way to turn. In the third place, Fannin with his expedition was at Goliad near Johnson and Grant. And Houston, the nominal commander of them all, was vainly trying to call back the Matamoras expeditions and to strengthen the garrison at San Antonio, where William B. Travis was now in command. As for the Mexicans, they were close at hand. On the 24th of February, Travis, whose force was concentrated at the Alamo, reported that Mexicans had occupied San Antonio across the river. The invaders at San Antonio proved to be the main Mexican army under command of Santa Anna in person. Three thousand Mexicans[1] were closing around one hundred and fifty Texans. But so unfaltering was the attitude of the Texans that one can sympathize with a great scholar of Texas when he calls "the letter in which Travis announced the opening of the siege the most heroic document among American historical records."

[1] The number is disputed. As this is the estimate of Professor E. C. Barker it may be considered authoritative.

COMMANDANCY OF THE ALAMO,
BEJAR, Feby. 24th, 1836 —

To the People of Texas & all Americans in the world:

FELLOW CITIZENS & COMPATRIOTS — I am besieged,
by a thousand or more of the Mexicans under Santa
Anna — I have sustained a continued Bombardment
& cannonade for 24 hours & have not lost a man —
the enemy has demanded a surrender at discretion,
otherwise, the garrison are to be put to the sword, if
the fort is taken — I have answered the demand with
a cannon shot, & our flag still waves proudly from the
walls — *I shall never surrender or retreat.   Then,* I call
on you in the name of Liberty, of patriotism, & everything dear to the American character, to come to our
aid, with all despatch — The enemy is receiving reinforcements daily & will no doubt increase to three or
four thousand in four or five days.   If this call is neglected, I am determined to sustain myself as long as
possible & die like a soldier who never forgets what
is due to his own honor & that of his country —
VICTORY OR DEATH.

WILLIAM BARRET TRAVIS
Lt. Col. comdt.

Of the three bodies of Texan soldiers — at San
Antonio, at Goliad, and at San Patricio — the one
farthest south was the first to meet disaster.   If a
Mexican column on the 24th of February had its
head against San Antonio, some part of it would
probably be within striking distance of San Patricio.

But the Texans lacked adequate information, and Johnson and Grant lingered at San Patricio, apparently without definite purpose. Suddenly the Mexicans fell upon them; their force was annihilated and Grant was killed. Though news of this disaster reached Fannin at Goliad, he continued to do nothing for another week. The Mexicans for once were more active than the Americans.

On the 1st of March, in the gray of the dawn, a little band of heroic men from Gonzales cut their way through the Mexican lines and brought to Travis their reënforcement. That same day the Texan Convention assembled at the town of Washington and was soon in possession of Travis' appeal. It named Houston commander-in-chief and urged him to go at once to the relief of Travis. On the 7th of March, Houston, who had attended the Convention, started for the front. He sent forward a dispatch ordering Fannin to join him on the way; but even then it was too late. The defense of the Alamo is now one of the classic episodes of American history. Before beginning the assault Santa Anna said to one of his generals: "You know that in this war there are no prisoners." One hundred and eighty-eight Anglo-Americans fought to the death against a Mexican force that outnumbered them sixteen to one. Not one of the Texans survived the storming. It was the proud Texan boast in after days that "Thermopylæ had its messenger of fate; the Alamo had none."

What happened inside the enclosure of the Alamo, on Sunday, the 6th of March, is known only from accounts of Mexican officers who took part in the storming, from the recollections of one American woman who spent the terrible hour of the combat in the convent church, and from the silent but superb eloquence of the death roll. Among many gallant men who went down with Travis two bore names that are bywords in American frontier tradition. James Bowie, brother of the Bowie who designed the perfect hunting knife, lay upon a cot, suffering from a recent injury, when the Mexican trumpets blew the signal, "no quarter," that Sunday morning. Nevertheless his death was a costly one for the Mexicans. David Crockett, who had come from his native Tennessee to throw in his lot with the Texans, sold his life amid the last massacre as grimly as a Norse Viking in an Icelandic saga. There had been another side to Crockett's heroism in the stern week when the Mexican trap was closing. He had the gift of music. His violin was the consolation of those men devoted to their own destruction while they waited for the end. Crockett, the dead shot, setting down his rifle, and smiting with his bow the strings of his violin, while nearer and nearer crept the encircling host of enemies — is there any finer instance of that figure which romance loves, the warrior-minstrel of the forlorn hope! The one woman of the garrison was the wife of Lieutenant Dickinson. With her little daughter she took refuge in the church while her husband fought furiously against the horde of cutthroats who poured in waves over the walls that surrounded the enclosure of the Alamo. Once, for an instant, he joined her, but only to cry out that the enemy were within the walls, and then after a parting kiss, to rush back sword in hand into the hopeless slaughter. "Soon after he left me," says Mrs. Dickinson, "three unarmed gunners came into the church and were shot down by my side. Just then a Mexican officer came in and asked me in English: 'Are you Mrs. Dickinson?' I answered, 'Yes.' 'Then,' said he, 'if you wish to save your life, follow me.' I followed him, and, although shot at and wounded, was spared."

The massacre at the Alamo intensified, it did not

create, a resolve for independence. Thus under the shadow of Santa Anna's approach the movement for independence reached its climax. It was the outcome of two diverse influences. During the winter the faction of Grant — possibly the faction of the speculators, of "tainted money," as we should say today — had steadily lost ground. Whether the tool of this faction or not, the Council had failed to lead the people. The Matamoras delusion had resulted in a Texas that was unprepared, with Santa Anna at its very gates. Then, too, there was another potent influence at work — the attitude of the United States, or rather of the people and of the money lenders of the United States. As to the people, no sooner was it learned that fighting had begun in Texas than volunteer companies were raised and started for the seat of war. At Cincinnati, for instance, a subscription was taken up to send artillery to Texas. Two cannon, afterward named the Twin Sisters, were cast by Miles Greenwood, a noted ironmaster of those days, and were dispatched to Texas, where they arrived in time to participate in the final victory and formed the whole of Houston's artillery train on the wild day of San Jacinto.

But the Government at Washington did not

commit itself. Though it is probable that Houston kept Jackson informed, the Administration preserved a careful neutrality. The money lenders followed a middle course. Austin found that he could borrow money for a prospective Texan republic but that American capital was cool toward aiding Texas as a province of Mexico. During the winter Austin had finally joined the party of independence. When the Convention met, virtually all Texas was at last of one mind. On the second day, the delegates solemnly and by unanimous vote declared Texas a free, sovereign, and independent republic. They then set to work upon a constitution and pending its adoption brushed aside Smith and the Council and established a new provisional government with David Burnet as President.

Five days after the fall of the Alamo, Houston arrived at Gonzales and, because of the terrible news he had just received from San Antonio changed his orders to Fannin, directing him to destroy Goliad and retreat to Victoria. Houston had no choice but to follow the same desperate course at Gonzales. Owing to the determination of each little group of volunteers to do what it pleased, such forces as Texas had — many of them

newly arrived volunteers from beyond the Sabine
— were scattered far apart. To order all to retreat
on converging lines; not to attempt a stand until
all were massed at one point; to choose a point
far enough away to preserve the start any group
possessed in the race with Santa Anna — such, as
any layman could see, was Houston's only chance
to assemble an army worth the name. To a born
soldier like Houston, no other course deserved a
minute's thought. During the next few weeks the
various Texan lines of retreat resembled roughly
the ribs of a fan along each of which a little Texan
force was falling back toward the northeast. Into
the midst of the fan a considerable Mexican army
was hurrying forward, intending to shatter the
portions and thus render insignificant the Texan army that would ultimately reach the point of
concentration.

It is reported that President Jackson at Washington, following with keen interest the Texan
retreat with the map of Texas before him, put his
finger on the spot that became the battlefield of
San Jacinto and said, "Here's the place. If Sam
Houston's worth one bawbee, he'll stand here and
give 'em a fight."

Houston proved himself "worth one bawbee"

and something more.   Before the day of his success
arrived, however, he had to overcome difficulties
scarcely to be measured.   What colored everything
else in those weeks was the flight of the whole
population eastward before Santa Anna, started by
Houston himself when he burned Gonzales.   At his
orders its people fled in any fashion they could,
their way lighted by the flames of their homes.
The narrative of a woman who took part in this
flight is worth all the retold accounts put together:

We camped the first night near Harrisburg.   Next day
we crossed Vince's Bridge and arrived at the San
Jacinto in the night.   There were fully five thousand
people at the ferry.   The planters from Brazoria and
Columbia with their slaves were crossing.   We waited
three days before we crossed. . . .   Every one was
trying to cross first, and it was almost a riot.

We got over on the third day, and after traveling a
few miles came to a big prairie.   It was about twelve
miles farther to the next timber and water, and some
of our party wanted to camp; but others said the
Trinity river was rising and if we delayed we might
not get across.   So we hurried on.   When we got about
half way across the prairie, Uncle Ned's wagon bogged.
The negro men driving the carts tried to go round the
big wagon one at a time until the four carts were fast
in the mud.   Mother was the only white woman that
rode in a cart; the others traveled on horseback.   Mrs.
Bell's four children, Mrs. Dyer's three, and Mother's

four rode in the carts. . . . The negro men put all the oxen to the wagon, but could not move it, so they had to stay there until morning. Mother gathered the white children in our cart. . . .

Mother with all the negro women and children walked six miles to the timber and found our friends in trouble. . . . The wagons and carts didn't get to the timber till night. They had to be unloaded and pulled out.

At the Trinity River men from the army began to join their families. I know they have been blamed for this but what else could they have done? The Texas army was retreating and the Mexicans were crossing the Colorado. Colonel Fannin and his men were prisoners, there were more negroes than whites among us and many of them were wild Africans, there was a large tribe of Indians on the Trinity as well as the Cherokee Indians in Eastern Texas at Nacogdoches, and there were tories, both Mexicans and Americans, in the country.[1]

While Houston was shepherding the now homeless Texans out of Gonzales, Fannin lost his final opportunity to serve his country. He had procrastinated and found excuses for not going to the Alamo, and now continued to defer action. He had not proper means of transport. He had sent out an officer with soldiers to gather in the

[1] *Reminiscences* of Mrs. Dilue Harris, in the *Quarterly* of the Texas State Historical Association, vol. iv, pp. 163–164.

population of the vicinity. He could not leave *him* behind and must send another force to hurry him up. There were other delays. The end of this trifling with responsibility was the destruction of all the companies in Fannin's jurisdiction. Some the Mexicans surprised and massacred. Others, including Fannin, surrendered, only to be shot in cold blood.

Meanwhile Houston amid the discontent of his men, whose families were fleeing under such desperate conditions continued the retreat. The "terrain," that is, the lay of the land, in eastern Texas reminds one of that in Venetia — a series of rivers running eastward through a region of plain and hill. And just as in 1918 we were all wondering at which river the Italians would stand against the inrushing Austrians, so in 1836 the question was at which river Santa Anna could be halted. Jackson read the signs correctly when he fixed upon the San Jacinto, which falls into a great indentation in Galveston Bay, as the point where topography and strategy favored a stand.

Santa Anna unwittingly helped on the inevitable by jumping to the conclusion that Texas lay at his mercy and by detaching parts of his army. His own march followed approximately the retreat of

Houston's immediate command until the 7th of April when the Mexicans entered San Felipe — or its ruins, for by this time the town had been burned. From San Felipe the opposing generals followed different courses as far as Harrisburg on Buffalo Bayou, which makes a right angle with the lower San Jacinto. The provisional government was sitting for the moment at Harrisburg. Thinking he might destroy this town at a blow, Santa Anna moved southward, crossed what must have seemed to him his last serious obstacle, the Brazos River, and then moved northeast upon Harrisburg. On the 15th of April he reached an empty town. Reports differ as to whether it was then on fire or was burned later on by Santa Anna. What had become of the Texan government? And where was Houston?

Santa Anna believed that Houston had taken a more circuitous route — as he had — but that he also had aimed at Harrisburg, and that his purpose was to pass through the town, follow Buffalo Bayou, then to cross the San Jacinto at Lynch's Ferry and continue eastward. In a word, Santa Anna thought he had beaten Houston in the race for Harrisburg and that all he now had to do was to push on, seize the San Jacinto ferry, and then turn

6

about and destroy Houston at his leisure. But he had not yet learned that he was dealing with a people very different from the Mexicans. The fiery Mexican was unable to gage the energetic American. The so-called fiery temperament forever confuses impulse and energy. Had Houston been a Mexican, Santa Anna would perhaps not have found his calculations so far beside the mark. He seems also to have thought Houston's army, if not already broken up, feeble enough to be destroyed by only a part of the Mexican forces.

For all these reasons Santa Anna felt safe in making the reckless move that was to prove his undoing. While his remaining forces were scattered in several directions, he pushed on with only seven hundred and fifty men toward New Washington, a village on Galveston Bay below the mouth of the San Jacinto. There he expected to capture the fleeing President of Texas, and yet to have plenty of time to reach the ferry before Houston. One of Santa Anna's outlying detachments under General Cos was also moving in the same direction along a route still farther south.

What had become of Houston while the enemy was thus advancing? He had abandoned San Felipe several days before the arrival of Santa

Anna. During the next three weeks while Santa Anna was passing him to the eastward his course presents problems, some of which have aroused sharp discussion. It is enough here to note that during this time he was swinging round a large curve northeast, then southeast, contending with the reckless spirit of his men, improving his organization, and at last striking the line of Santa Anna's march on the Buffalo Bayou on Monday, the 18th of April. Santa Anna had passed by the day before on his march to New Washington. Thus Santa Anna's miscalculations began to work his undoing. Unsuspected, the enemy whom he thought he could deal with at his leisure was close behind him, as he marched on in high spirits to New Washington. Not finding his prey at New Washington, he amused himself by burning the town and then resumed his serious business — the trapping of Houston by the seizure of the San Jacinto ferry.

Meanwhile Houston had captured a Mexican courier and thus learned of Santa Anna's plans. He determined to spring a trap and hurried forward along the south shore of Buffalo Bayou. On the morning of the 20th of April, both generals were marching on the same point, the San Jacinto ferry.

Santa Anna, coming up from New Washington, was moving northward with his seven hundred and fifty men. Houston, with about seven hundred and eighty, was moving eastward. The Texans reached the point of vantage first and there they encamped in a live-oak grove and waited. At their backs was the bayou, a narrow but deep stream that joined the San Jacinto at the ferry about half a mile distant. It was a lovely spot, for the high banks of the bayou were covered with oaks, huge magnolias eighty feet high, and great masses of laurel, bay, and rhododendron. Southward of the wood where the Texans camped was a stretch of prairie. Watching this open space, the hardy, adventurous Texans, each a dead shot, lay beneath the great canopy of the silvery gray-green live oak boughs, straining their eyes into the sun-glare of the prairie, counting the hours before the Mexicans should appear.

Early in the day Santa Anna's scouts informed him that Houston had already arrived. "It was with the greatest joy," says Santa Anna, "that all the individuals belonging to the corps then under my immediate orders heard the news, and they continued the march, already begun in the best spirit." Skirmishing later in the day, designed to draw Houston out of the wood into the open, failed of its purpose. Santa Anna therefore pitched his camp on an eminence about a thousand yards from the wood of the Texans. There he constructed breastworks. Early next morning General Cos joined Santa Anna, increasing his force to something like twelve hundred men. Thursday, the 21st of April, wore on without a demonstration from either side. Fearing that more Mexican reenforcements were on their way, a band of Texans led by "Deaf" Smith, a figure famous in Texan tradition, destroyed a bridge which spanned Vince's Creek, a tributary of the San Jacinto, over which additions to the Mexican force would almost certainly pass. Then in the late afternoon Houston's army, screened by their oak trees, began silently to prepare for battle. Again Santa Anna underrated his opponents. Still unaware of the manner of man he had to deal with, the Mexican general went to sleep. His army neglected to take the most obvious precautions. Their horses were unsaddled. The men were busy cooking. Suddenly at the edge of the grove of live oaks, a thousand yards away, appeared a line of men. A solitary fife struck up, "Will you come to the bower I have shaded for you?" Immediately the

Texan battle line swept out into the open and forward on the run. Now they were shouting, "Remember the Alamo!" All the fury of revenge nursed during the terrible days of the retreat rang in those fierce shouts and in the tempest of rifle fire that followed. A few Mexicans stood for a moment at the breastwork. Then all broke and fled, while the Texans shot them like running game. Thus ended Santa Anna's confident expedition. The Texan loss was but two killed and twenty-three wounded; of the Mexican army scarcely forty escaped death, wounds, or capture. Houston reported the dead alone at over six hundred. A miserable fugitive brought in the next day proved to be Santa Anna.

CHAPTER V

THE war which began at Gonzales in 1835 did not end until the Treaty of Guadalupe-Hidalgo, thirteen years later. It forms part of the background and at times invades the foreground of American history all through these eventful years. It was an intermittent war, it is true, but it unifies the period of thirteen years over which it cast its shadow.

The details of Texan experience during these years — the constitution making, the local politics, the financial desperation — form an interesting but not a unique story, and hardly have a place on the broad page of American history. The first commission sent by Texas to the United States returned despondent, with the report that the American Government stood neutral and that money could be raised only by pledging Texas land at cruelly low figures. A second and third commission were sent to organize American sympathy. But nothing came of these efforts except glowing reports of American intentions and the reiteration of the belief of the commissioners that President Jackson favored the cause of the Texans. The fact that this bluntest of men would not come out frankly on the subject does not seem to have impressed them.

In 1836 the scene shifts to Washington, where the fate of Texas was ultimately decided. Jackson was then as eager to extend his dominion to the Rio Grande as he had been in 1829 or in 1835. But it was a bad time to spring new issues on the American public. Jackson the somewhat misty imperialist might relish the idea of presenting to his countrymen a great domain bought and paid for by his astuteness alone; on the other hand Jackson the politician was very cautious about involving the country in war on the eve of a presidential election. The first Texan commission had evoked from him only a rhetorical flourish about the obligations of the United States to Mexico. During 1836 Jackson's rôle continued to be that of a strict preserver of neutrality. And yet for a brief time during that year United States troops were on Texan soil — or, as Mexico maintained, Mexican soil. General Gaines had been ordered southwest to see that no

military force, either Texan or Mexican, violated
the neutral territory of the United States. For
some time Gaines lay encamped with a small force
on the east bank of the Sabine. He was there when
the battle of San Jacinto took place, and an old
fiction, now obsolete, explained his presence at that
point as part of Jackson's secret support of the
Texan revolution. But while Jackson was not
actually abetting the revolution, no one with any
knowledge of his character can doubt that events
might have taken place in which — presidential
election or no presidential election — all Jackson's
political opportunism would have vanished, and he
would have plunged the United States into war.
Had the battle of the San Jacinto proved a rout
for the Texans, had the host of fleeing non-com-
batants reached the Sabine, it is as nearly certain as
anything unproven ever can be that Jackson would
have stalked in between Santa Anna and his prey.

It was partly, we may believe, to protect the
fleeing Texans even if Santa Anna did not overtake
them, that Gaines and his army were at the Sabine.
While Houston was gathering all he could of the
man power of Texas for his stand against Santa
Anna, the fleeing settlers were exposed to the alter-
nate horror of attack by the Indians. Gaines was

instructed, if he saw danger of an Indian outbreak, to cross the Sabine and attack the Indians. Though he did not advance previous to Houston's victory, a report that the Indians were rising led Gaines briefly to occupy Nacogdoches in the summer of 1836. In consequence the Mexican Minister, after a sharp controversy, demanded his passport and withdrew from Washington in October.

In the six months since Houston's victory, Jackson had been studying the trend of events. There was, indeed, much to think upon during the six months which ended in the withdrawal of the Mexican Minister. First of all there were the debates in Congress. When Senator Thomas Morris of Ohio, as early as April, presented a petition from citizens of Cincinnati "on the subject of the struggle for freedom now going on in Texas, and suggesting the expediency of acknowledging the independence of that country," he stirred up a hornet's nest. All the great leaders of the day took part in the violent discussion which followed. Out of the turmoil of debate at least one fact emerged unmistakably: Congress did not want to enter the war. John C. Calhoun of South Carolina, indeed, though seeing plainly that annexation of Texas meant war, pressed not only for recognition, but for annexation. But many politicians anticipated the position which Preston, Calhoun's colleague, took a year later when he said that, much as he wanted Texas, he would not annex it until its independence of Mexico was past dispute. From the latter point of view the actions of Gaines were suspicious to say the least. John Quincy Adams, during a debate in May, openly charged the Administration with having sent Gaines to the border with the purpose of involving the United States in the war.

At first, the discussion did not reveal either sectional or slavery bias. Senator Morris not only presented the first petition for recognizing Texas but soon after presented various anti-slavery petitions. The only State whose legislature sent in resolutions favoring recognition was Connecticut. Some of the bitterest of the early opposition to annexation was voiced by Senator Porter of Louisiana, who maintained that the war was ruining the trade of his State with Mexico and that, if Texas was annexed, Mexican raids would soon extend to Louisiana. "It is all very well," he maintained, "for gentlemen who come from States where peace and security would not be disturbed by hostilities to indulge in aspirations after the happiness of the human race." But he protested against their doing so at Louisiana's expense. The upshot of this war debate was a report by the Committee on Foreign Relations of which Henry Clay was chairman. The document was blandly non-committal and came to the conclusion "that the independence of Texas ought to be acknowledged by the United States" whenever Texas was independent. This smooth evasion of the crucial point was quite like Clay.

The keen old President and his ring of astute advisers — "practical" politicians of the true blood — saw all this discussion in a perspective that is sometimes forgotten. Jackson was only just then extricating himself from a serious European predicament caused by too hastily joining issue with France, on the assumption that the Americans were in a warlike mood. Throughout these months of 1836, when the fate of the politicians was in the balance, the United States was without a minister at Paris, and there was no French minister at Washington. The rupture in diplomatic relations had taken place in the previous year. In attempting to make an end of those French spoliation claims outstanding since Napoleon, Jackson had tried a show of force and had issued mobilization orders to the American navy. But the American people were equivocal, to say the least, in their attitude on the subject. Clay had got a unanimous vote in the Senate for resolutions to the effect that the President had exceeded his authority. Calhoun had warned the country that it was drifting into war with France through the haste and violence of the President. Late in 1835 Jackson's advisers were urging him to draw in his horns. A circumstance which the Texan commissioners in the first half of 1836 failed to note was the studied attempt of the Administration to withdraw from the belligerent attitude of the previous year. The American people were quick to respond. It was the new tone of the President's dealing with France that led Washington Irving in February, 1836, to write to Van Buren expressing his delight. The credit for the change Irving attributed altogether to Van Buren. He was the pacific wizard behind the throne. It was he upon whom the Texas envoy at Washington ultimately laid the blame for the defeat of all the schemes to recognize Texas in 1836. "I have made it my business to unravel the mystery," he wrote, "and I know I have succeeded. . . . It all proceeds from Mr. Van Buren's party. . . . They are afraid of throwing Mr. Van Buren into a minority in the next Congress."

When regarded in the perspective of the political campaign of 1836, the evasiveness of the Administration ceases to be mysterious. "Old Hickory" had always admired the political adroitness of Van Buren and had set his heart upon making him the next President. But there were obstacles in the way. The first half of 1836 brought the climax of Jackson's financial battle in the distribution of the surplus among the States. He had in solid array against him all the financial interests of the country. And in the great commonwealth of New York, so often the deciding State in presidential elections, factions had so rent the party that promoters of Van Buren were greatly alarmed. And now there was still another source of alarm. Though the Texas question entered politics without a sectional bias, it speedily became entangled both with sectionalism and with slavery. Senator Morris of Ohio, the anti-slavery advocate who was its sponsor in the Senate, before long began to cool. The indomitable John Quincy Adams sounded an anti-slavery rallying cry. On the 25th of May he denounced the Administration as conspiring to reestablish slavery on soil where it had been abolished and as scheming to force the United States into the war in the interest of the slaveholders. So violent was Adams in his language that, in the reaction of the next day, he pronounced his speech "the most hazardous" he had ever made. But in a way it was less hazardous and more strategic than he supposed. Later he wrote in his diary that the North greeted it with "a universal shout of applause." Through such troubled waters the ship of Van Buren's political fortune — with Jackson in command, if not quite at the helm — was laboring toward a perilous haven beyond the November election.

It had been reiterated in congressional debates that no one had enough certain knowledge about Texan conditions to warrant decisive action. Was it to forestall any complaint by friends of Texas that Jackson sent Henry M. Morfit on a mission of inquiry? Did he hope to find Texas so strong that he might use the knowledge as a trump, should the cards begin to run against Van Buren, or was he honestly seeking light without ulterior purpose? The biographers of Jackson have left us in the dark as to his motive. Whatever it was, Morfit went on his mission, and in August and September, while the American voters in high revel took their fill of electioneering, he wrote letter after letter to the State

Department describing Texas. It was a discouraging picture that he painted. The army was unstable.
The population consisted of some thirty thousand
Americans, five thousand negroes, and thirty-five
hundred Mexicans, as well as twelve or fourteen
thousand independent Indians. Though the Texas
leaders had meditated conquering everything between them and the Pacific, they had decided to
make the Rio Grande their western boundary as far
north as its source. This extension would give them
part of the province of New Mexico and fifteen thousand additional population. But New Mexico was
not yet conquered. Financially the new republic
presented a curious spectacle.. It was deep in debt
and yet had conducted a successful war with "little
embarrassment to her citizens or her treasury";
this by no means insignificant accomplishment was
due to the bountiful inflow of donations from the
United States. Morfit concluded that Texas would
be little likely to maintain its independence since
"without foreign aid her future security must de-
pend more upon the weakness and imbecility of
her enemy than upon her own strength."

Morfit probably had no great insight into men
and nations. It is hard to say what weight his
reports had. A personal letter from Houston to

Jackson may have accomplished more. Houston was even more pessimistic then Morfit. He acknowledged that the Texan situation was desperate, so long as Mexico was determined to continue the war, and he begged his old friend Jackson to come to his assistance. But in 1836 Jackson had other fish to fry, and perhaps he had some real faith in the singular, not to say grotesque, performance of Santa Anna's captors.

The majority of his captors wanted to give Santa Anna an expeditious hanging, but Houston and Burnet managed to save his life. Then they made him sign a treaty which bound him not to take up arms against Texas "during the present war of independence," bound the Mexican forces to withdraw across the Rio Grande, and provided that Santa Anna himself should be allowed to return to Mexico. A secret article promised the recognition of the independence of Texas and by implication the Rio Grande as a boundary.

How Burnet and Houston could have taken this so-called treaty seriously — knowing Santa Anna as they did — is a mystery. Later Santa Anna publicly declared his part of the negotiation a mere device for making his escape from Texas. As might have been expected, Mexico struck the bottom out

7

of the treaty by enacting that any agreement made by the President while a prisoner should "be regarded as null, void, and of no effect." A meeting of Texan soldiers prevented the return of Santa Anna to his own country and very nearly put an end to his life. Thereupon Santa Anna was induced to write to Jackson begging him to employ his influence to put the treaty into effect. Jackson returned an answer that was unimpeachable from the point of view of international law and as cool as if his beloved Texans were subjects of the Emperor of Cathay. He deeply regretted that the whole affair was beyond his competence, unless Mexico should officially request his good offices. This was in September and the presidential election was not yet won.

During that same month the first regular election was held in the Republic of Texas. Houston was elected President, and the new constitution drawn up by the convention was ratified by the people. But far more significant was the plebiscite which recorded some six thousand Texan voters in favor of annexation to the United States and only ninety-three opposed to it. One of the early acts of the new Government was the dispatch of William F. Wharton from the still unrecognized republic as Minister to the United States and the almost simultaneous release of Santa Anna so that he too as informal ambassador might intercede for Texas.

With the election of Van Buren to the presidency Jackson ceases to be the leading man in the tragi-comedy of the Texan negotiations. His course for the next two months is far from clear, but it is no longer of chief importance. The dealings with Santa Anna, as might have been expected, came to nothing. The only person who gained anything by the farce was Santa Anna himself. With delicious effrontery he asked the President for a warship to take him home, and it was given him! Has history any picture more ironical than that of this butcher of the Alamo, protected by Texan statesmen from the wrath of their soldiers, politely released from the country, politely bowing himself out of Washington, and escorted to the deck of an American warship, whereby he was conveyed in safety to his native land!

At Washington the center of gravity in the Texan negotiation now changed from the White House to the Capitol. Apparently Jackson's aim was to shift the responsibility for Texas upon Congress. Ostentatiously he announced that he would let Congress guide him in this great matter. When Jackson consented to be guided, there was always a reason for his docility; but he was the last man in such a situation to make candid confession of his reasons. Perhaps the guesses of the Texan Minister are as safe a guide as any to Jackson's wishes and purposes. His confidential correspondence with his government shows Jackson eager for annexation but unwilling to take the lead. He intimates that the President encouraged him to make an extravagant claim to all northern Mexico, even to the Pacific, so as to give annexation a national rather than a sectional interest, and he concludes that Jackson's main purpose in all this deviousness was to avoid making enemies for Van Buren in the next Congress. Be that as it may, the friends of Texas in the Congress which met for its last session in December, that month of good omen, determined to bring things to a head. In spite of all the talk about annexation, they decided to reopen the fight on the narrower question of recognition. A Senate resolution that the Republic of Texas should be recognized called forth the eloquent support of Calhoun and the temporizing opposition of Clay. On March 1, 1837, the resolution was adopted.

A more practical device in favor of Texas was the work of Waddy Thompson of South Carolina in the House of Representatives. He moved to amend the civil and diplomatic appropriation bill so as to provide for "a diplomatic agent to be sent to the independent republic of Texas." The House struck out the word "independent" and made the appointment conditional upon the President's receiving "satisfactory evidence that Texas is an independent power." In this form both Houses passed the recommendation and thereby adroitly threw back upon Jackson the responsibility which he had tried to fix on them. But this time he accepted the responsibility, though his precise motive remains obscure. He sent for Wharton and some other Texans to have a glass of wine with him on the night of the 3d of March. That day, he told them, he had nominated a chargé d'affaires to the Republic of Texas. He had said to Congress that he regarded its action as "a virtual decision of the question," and that it was his duty to acquiesce therein.

But the recognition of the Republic of Texas was only the prelude to the real play. The fundamental issue was still annexation. A breathing space, however, followed the recognition. It was now plain that on the larger issue the political lines would be sharply drawn. Wharton perceived the coming storm. He wrote home that it would "agitate this union more than did the attempt to restrict Missouri, nullification, and abolitionism, all combined." An ominous sign was the political composition of the new Congress. Though the Administration had a majority in both Houses, the Whigs, in opposition, showed a dangerous increase over the previous Congress. When James K. Polk, the previous Speaker of the House, was reëlected, it was by a margin of only thirteen votes.

The trial of strength in Congress between friends and foes of annexation was postponed by the terrible business collapse known as the panic of 1837. But even while the country staggered on the edge of ruin, while Whigs and Democrats were defining their relation to a catastrophe of the first magnitude, the indefatigable Texan agents went on log-rolling for annexation. Memucan Hunt, who had succeeded Wharton, sought in vain to enlist the support of the Administration. President Van Buren refused to turn aside from what he deemed the larger issues. With the business of the country prostrate, the danger of inciting war with Mexico by annexing Texas could not be incurred. When Hunt, in August, made a formal application to the State Department on behalf of Texas for permission to enter the Union, the Secretary bluntly told him that he was inviting the United States to enter into a war. "So long as Texas shall remain at war, while the United States are at peace with her adversary, the proposition of the Texan minister plenipotentiary necessarily involves the question of war with that adversary."

Hunt appears to have considered the attitude of the Administration as political chicanery. He did not appreciate the reluctance of all the business interests of the country to be drawn into war at such a time. But he was quite right in seeing the whole episode in the terms of politics, especially since friends of Texas who had the confidence of Van Buren assured him that the Democratic leaders dared not "jeopardize the strength of the party in the North by precipitate action on the subject."

During 1837 two events took place in the United States the importance of which the Texans did not fully realize. In the first place, the anti-slavery agitation reached a point of acute crisis. In the previous year John Quincy Adams had joined the abolitionists and had become their chief voice in Congress. The suppression by the House of the

right of petition on the subject of slavery had made
Congress a boiling pot with the lid clamped down.
In November, 1837, one of the great tragedies of
the anti-slavery crusade took place. The abolitionist Lovejoy was murdered by a mob in Illinois.
The cold fury aroused in men like Adams by this
outrage is beyond description. They set out to be
revenged on the whole party of slaveholders.

In this year, too, abolitionists reached a definite
conviction that the annexation of Texas was identified with the interests of slavery. The idea of a
conspiracy of slaveholders and annexationists orig-
inated with Benjamin Lundy, when that famous
abolitionist in 1832 devised his scheme for plant-
ing free colonies in Texas. Had his plans material-
ized, Texas would have been — like Kansas a quarter century later — a labyrinth of hostile colonies,
some free, some slave. Although the plan was
never carried out, Lundy made several visits to
Texas and Mexico, and fell in with a notorious
Colonel Almonte, the bosom friend of Santa Anna,
who appears to have filled him with the Mexican
view of Texas. Lundy came home convinced that
Texas was a den of thieves. He wrote articles
for the abolitionist newspapers and published two
pamphlets, *The Origin and True Cause of the Texas*

Insurrection and *The War in Texas*, in which the
violence of his language was matched by the in-
accuracy of his knowledge. He looked upon the
war as an "invasion of brigands from the United
States" who had the "avowed purpose of adding
five or six more slaveholding States to this Union."
Lundy's views were taken over bodily by Adams.
Remembering that these were largely the views of
Almonte and that through Adams they were foisted
upon historians for half a century, we have here
one more instance of the perversion of history by
uncritical writers. By the end of 1837 sectional
prejudice and anti-slavery passion had produced a
new political force hostile to Texas and fiercely
uncompromising.

In December, the enemies of Texas forced the
fighting. The moment of attack was well chosen.
The dread of war, with American business still
prostrate, was widespread. Even among some of
the slavery champions this dread outweighed the
desire to acquire Texas. It had inspired Governor
McDuffie of South Carolina, in the most singular
act of his life, to urge the South Carolina Legislature to reconsider their "almost unanimously
expressed desire" for the admission of Texas, giving as his reason that it would promptly involve

the United States in the war and would lead to servile insurrections in Louisiana and the neighboring States. Another strategic feature of the moment was the composition of Congress. Though Texas was not yet definitely a party issue, the Whigs, who were the champions of business against the *laissez-faire* policy of the Administration, could be trusted to stand pat against war. The Administration forces, with their narrow majority of only thirteen and with business not yet restored, would hardly have the courage, even if they had the wish, to hold together on a policy that involved war. Furthermore, the Administration had been busy during 1837 seeking to adjust a long list of claims of American citizens against Mexico. At the close of the year these claims were in sight of arbitration. Diplomatic relations had been resumed. A Mexican Minister had reached Washington. Annexation and war would throw aside the hope of any profitable settlement. Instead of some crumb of financial solace in Mexican payments, there would be that necessity of all wars — taxes. The enemies of annexation seemed likely at this critical moment to score a moral victory by squarely meeting and rejecting the project.

The issue was brought before Congress when

Senator Benjamin Swift of Vermont presented resolutions by his State Legislature condemning the proposal to annex Texas. Instantly the issue was accepted as a sectional battle. After the reading of the Vermont resolutions, Senator William R. King of Alabama pronounced them "an infamous libel and insult on the South." Calhoun deemed the present moment one of the greatest importance; a great step had been taken in the progress of events; he had long foreseen the present state of things, and now the time had actually come when it was to be determined whether we were to remain longer as one united and happy people, or whether this blessed union was to be dissolved by the hand of violence; Vermont had struck a deep and dangerous blow into the vitals of our confederacy. Swift withdrew the resolutions for that day but gave notice that he would bring them up again.

Then Calhoun with his usual courage, believing that an issue might as well be met at its first appearance, accepted the gage of battle. On the 27th of December he gave his counterblast to the Vermont resolutions. Though Texas was not named, the view of the Union and of the situation of the moment, as shown in the Calhoun resolutions, made the attempt to exclude Texas seem an impertinence, not to say a treason. On January 4, 1838, his colleague, William C. Preston, advanced the discussion to its permanent form. In a set of resolutions he asked the Senate to denounce the Treaty of 1819 under which the region between the Sabine and the Rio Grande had been "surrendered"; and urged that "whenever it can be effected consistently with the faith and treaty stipulations of the United States, it is desirable and expedient to annex the said Territory to the United States."

Thus the Congressional battle began. In the course of the struggle which raged for six months, Preston made the declaration that he did not contemplate annexation until Mexico could be brought to consent and that he was not trying to involve the United States in war. Perhaps this admission cut the ground from under him. At least the strategists of the attack had gaged the situation correctly. By degrees an anti-Texas coalition was formed. In June Preston's resolutions were tabled.

In the House the coalition had harder work and came much nearer to defeat. Again Waddy Thompson was the pro-Texan leader. The counter-attack was directed by Adams. He fought with all the controlled fierceness and deadly precision that made him second to none in the bitterness of debate. His final move was a famous piece of obstruction. During three weeks, from the 16th of June to the end of the session, he held the free time of the House in a continuing speech. Thus Adams killed a resolution fathered by Thompson and similar in character to the resolutions of Preston. This famous "Texas Speech," as it is now known, was afterward enlarged and published. It contained a review of Texan history which was taken up by historians and has endured until our own day.

CHAPTER VI

THE MEXICAN SHADOW

DURING ten years the Republic which was proclaimed at Washington-on-the-Brazos on March 2, 1836, watched with troubled eyes a great shadow upon the southern horizon. To the student of to-day the shadow seems indeed but a shadow; but to the men of that day it was not yet certain that the Mexican peril lacked substance. It is surprising that the danger was not terribly real. Texas was very sparsely settled. Its little homesteads and towns were separated by great spaces. It was just the country to invite raiders, for it afforded to the predatory horseman rich opportunity. He might choose his own time and course and might destroy a settlement, even far within the border, and escape, with only a handful of his enemies informed of his movements. All that saved Texas in these perilous days was the amazing slowness and stupidity of the Mexicans. Had the Texans faced rovers of the type of the Tatars, or the Six Nations, their worst alarm would have been justified.

The second President of Texas, Mirabeau Bonaparte Lamar, whose extraordinary name fitted the visionary idealism of his character, seems to have had in him enough of the poet to spoil the statesman. In December, 1838, Lamar succeeded Houston — for the Texan constitution forbade the President to succeed himself — and began at once the ambitious attempt to make Texas a great independent power. Taking advantage of the natural reaction away from the United States, Lamar gave free scope to his visionary temperament, and for a time Texas followed him. Of the various ill-judged measures which he devised only one needs to be mentioned here. That one the Texan Congress refused to sanction, whereupon Lamar put it through on his own responsibility. It was nothing less than an attempt to break up the trade which then flourished between Mexico and the United States through Santa Fé and to compel this trade to take a new course southward through Texas. Neither the precise rights of a neutral in trade with a belligerent, nor the nice distinctions of international law seem to have occurred to this dreamer President. Even had his mad attempt succeeded, the resulting complications with the United States would doubtless have confused him; but it was a tragic failure. The men in the feeble expedition which he sent against Santa Fé suffered frightful hardship, reached New Mexico in a starving condition, and were easily overpowered and taken prisoner. The only material effect of this disastrous foray was to inflame Mexico and assure renewal of the war at the earliest opportunity.

The Santa Fé tragedy destroyed the popularity of Lamar, and Houston was acclaimed as his successor. What Lamar had sown Houston now had to reap. Coming into office in December, 1841, he had not long to wait for the Mexican counterstroke. In March, 1842, a Mexican army, taking advantage of the lay of the land to make a secret advance, suddenly appeared before San Antonio. Simultaneously raiding parties swept over the southern horizon and fell upon other Texan towns. But this first onrush was not an invasion in force; loot was its principal object. Having seized what they could carry off, the Mexicans vanished as suddenly as they had appeared.

Exaggerated reports of the raid swept over Texas and reached the United States, where an adventurous sympathy with Texas again became the

fashion of the moment. Volunteers set out for the
scene of danger, and a militia force assembled in
Texas. But Houston had no mind for a premature
stroke by unorganized forces and during the summer the militia melted away. In September, when
the ordinary routine of life was going on at San
Antonio, the judge of the district holding court,
the leading members of the bar arguing before him,
a Mexican force of some twelve hundred men,
under General Adrian Woll, descended on the town.
After a little sharp fighting, these Mexicans swept
away southward, carrying off a number of prisoners,
including the leading members of the San Antonio
bar and the judge himself.

This second San Antonio raid again aroused in
Texas fierce discussions of what ought to be done.
Again volunteers flocked together and demanded
a counter invasion of Mexico. Again Houston
tried to prevent a premature stroke and sought to
persuade the impatient people to form some sort of
effective military organization. But neither President nor people would accept the other's plan, and
while they wrangled, the Texan forces again began
to melt away. Thereupon three hundred enthusiasts resolved to take things into their own hands.
They elected a commander, made their way across

8

the Rio Grande, and attacked the Mexican town of Mier on Christmas Day, 1842. It so happened that Mier was at that moment occupied by a Mexican force which outnumbered the Texans probably four to one. Though the invaders fought furiously in the streets of Mier, their battle was hopeless from the beginning. On the afternoon of the next day the few Texans who remained surrendered upon written assurance from the Mexican commander that they should be treated "with the consideration which is in accordance with the magnanimous Mexican nation."

While on the march to the Mexican capital in February, 1843, these Mier prisoners overpowered their guard and made their escape. Seeking safety in the neighboring mountains, they lost their way and suffered horribly for want of food. Some died of starvation, and those who survived were at length recaptured. As a punishment for their hardihood, every tenth man was shot. The rest were sent to the dungeons of the castle of Perote, where many died, so that in the end only a pitiful handful remained to be liberated.

Such, in the opening months of 1843, was the desperate military situation in which Houston found himself. His diplomatic outlook was equally dark. Early in the previous fateful year Houston had renewed overtures with a view to annexing Texas to the United States. But Daniel Webster, who was then Secretary of State, was an enemy of Texas and gave him no encouragement. He was scarcely cordial upon the subject of mediation between Texas and Mexico, though at length he consented to act if England and France coöperated. When he heard of the Mier expedition, however, he told the Texan Minister at Washington that he would have nothing further to do with mediation.

Meanwhile a strange performance on the part of an erratic officer of the United States Navy promised for a moment to bring Webster over to Houston's side, though in the end it made the breach between them wider than ever. We shall hear later of certain acrid notes that passed between Washington and Mexico City because Webster persisted, to the disgust of the Mexicans, in an attitude of strict neutrality. To the Mexican mind, as to the later German mind, neutrality was not a legal status but an emotional condition. When Webster, keeping strictly to international law, would not play the hand of Mexico, the Mexican Minister of Foreign Affairs issued statements that seemed to indicate the beginning of hostilities.

These remarks came to the ears of Commodore Jones, who commanded a small squadron of American ships then off the coast of Peru, and, together with certain absurd and groundless rumors, aroused his patriotism to the boiling point. Setting all sail, he made for the coast of Mexico, confident that before he sighted its shores the two countries would be deep in a great war. When he arrived before Monterey, California, the Commodore did not pause to question the basis of his judgment but at once invested the town. Imagine the bewilderment of the inhabitants who were thus compelled to produce newspapers and various other evidence in an effort to persuade this strange impetuous man from the sea that Mexico and the United States were at peace.

This amazing farce occurred in October of 1842. It became known at Washington in January, 1843. Thereupon John Quincy Adams, the most relentless of the enemies of Texas, again took up the cudgels against her. It had leaked out that President Tyler differed from his Secretary of State in desiring a revival of the issue of Texan annexation, which had become increasingly likely during the latter part of 1842. Adams, now heart and soul the anti-slavery leader and always on the *qui vive* to discover a Southern plot on behalf of slavery, watched every item of news with a bitter and prejudiced eye, for he was utterly suspicious of Tyler. To Adams this news of what Jones had done meant but one thing. Somehow, somewhere, a scheme was on foot to embroil the United States with Mexico and to force the country into a war on behalf of slaveholding Texas. As for Jones, he had stupidly bungled the matter. Even when the Administration promptly recalled Jones and disavowed his action, Adams was not satisfied. He wanted Jones disgraced. Nothing short of that would prove the good faith of the Administration, though Tyler in a message to Congress stated that Jones had acted "entirely of his own authority."

So lacking in temperate judgment were Adams and his close associates that they presently issued an *Address to the People of the Free States*. This paper revealed the same absolute satisfaction with a personal sense of evidence that had inspired the conduct of the erratic Jones. Its thirteen signers declared positively that the Southern States were conspiring to annex Texas in order that "the undue ascendency of the slaveholding power of the Government shall be secured and riveted beyond all redemption." After a long review of all the charges originally inspired by Almonte and Lundy, the *Address* advanced to new ground in an audacious threat that the annexation of Texas would justify the free States in dissolving the Union.

The *Address* was dated March 3, 1843, the day on which Congress adjourned. On the same day the Senate altered a Treaty of Commerce and Amity which Webster after long delays had consented to negotiate with the Texan Republic. The alterations made the treaty unacceptable to Texas. Thus in the spring of 1843 Houston came to a point where his situation appeared desperate. Despite the rumors of a new movement of annexation, the United States Department of State was still in the hands of the great political genius who was his enemy. The implacable Adams, who had once defeated annexation, was openly moving for an anti-Texan combination that should stop at nothing before its goal. The military events since the resumption of hostilities were all in favor of Mexico. The tragedy of the Mier prisoners was in every mind. And this state of things had been brought about while Santa Anna, again the hero of Mexico, was engaged in a civil war with the province of Yucatan. What might happen should Santa Anna prevail, or should a compromise be effected with Yucatan, and all the power of the Mexican government be turned against Texas?

There was, however, still one card in Houston's hand which had not been played. We must turn now to his relations with England.

CHAPTER VII

ENGLAND AS PEACEMAKER

THE story of Texas is full of strange historical parallels and apparent anticipations, as if the shadows of coming events were ominously cast before. We have seen that Benjamin Lundy in Texas would have anticipated John Brown in Kansas. Curiously, too, the same boisterous Palmerston of England, who had to deal with the question of recognition of Texas, was embarrassed twenty years later by that of recognizing the Confederacy. Palmerston was probably as well disposed toward an independent Texas as he was toward the Confederacy in the later years when the caprice of fortune had again inflicted him upon the English people. But he had no more intention of pulling some one else's chestnuts out of the fire in the one case than in the other. He held off, waiting to see what Texas could do by herself, and carried water on both shoulders by agreeing that a Texan ship might go into "the Ports of Great Britain as a Mexican ship, according to the stipulations of the Mexican treaty, notwithstanding that the Documents used for such ship should bear upon their face that they were the avowed act of a government in Texas, assuming the style of a Republic independent of Mexico."

While Palmerston thus held off from an honest recognition, Texas tried without success to borrow money in England and France. The failure was due to various influences. The gigantic collapse of American business in the panic of 1837 was fresh in every mind, and Europe was still wary of all transatlantic investments. Many Englishmen had already burned their fingers lending money to Mexico and they feared that any financial support of Texas might cause a further decrease in the value of their Mexican bonds. Furthermore — a significant fact — the British and Foreign Anti-slavery Society was opposed to the creation of a new slaveholding power. Thus early the slavery question became a factor in Texan diplomacy.

It was the slave trade, indeed, which in part at least persuaded Palmerston to recognize Texas. The British people were eager to have their navy sweep the slaver from the seas. But to accomplish this end it was necessary to possess a treaty-right to visit, if not to search, ships flying other flags than the Union Jack. In trying to persuade the United States to grant such a right, Palmerston used the bullying tone natural to him and offended the old sensitiveness of Americans over the right of search. The American ambassador at London, Andrew Stevenson, gave Palmerston as good as he got by serving notice that, in the absence of a definite treaty granting it, no claim to the right of search would be tolerated at Washington. Then the American Secretary of State informed the British Government that his country would not accept a treaty giving right of search to British cruisers. But in spite of this opposition, Palmerston turned the flank of the United States by agreeing in 1840 to recognize Texas as a new republic upon the condition that it allow a mutual right of search by cruisers of the two powers in suppressing the slave trade. But Texas hesitated at the right of search, and for two years the agreement remained unratified.

Meanwhile a curious coincidence occurred. Almost at the same time the administrations changed in Texas, in the United States, in Mexico, and in England. In 1841, Houston became President of

Texas a second time, Webster became Secretary of State for the United States, Santa Anna returned to power in Mexico, and in London, Palmerston was succeeded at the Foreign Office by the Earl of Aberdeen.

The new Foreign Secretary in England found a transatlantic situation of many complications. As to Mexico, there were the clamorous British bond-holders ever ready to denounce him should he provoke that unstable nation into a frank repudiation of its debts. To avoid a rupture with Mexico was therefore an enforced item in his policy. The quarrel between Maine and Canada over their boundary line had culminated in recent border tumults now called the "Aroostook War" and for a time had seemed to threaten the gravest consequences. To settle the Maine-Canada dispute was a pressing part of Aberdeen's American policy. Moreover, the long standing Oregon question must not longer be neglected. Finally, there was Texas. The treaty recognizing its independence, conditional on the right of search in suppression of the slave trade, was still unratified.

The question of slavery was undoubtedly close to Aberdeen's heart. Before the close of 1841, before he had been a year in office, he negotiated the now famous Quintuple Treaty under which France, England, Russia, Prussia, and Austria adopted uniform laws with regard to the slave trade and gave to one another a limited right of search. On the day the treaty was signed Aberdeen wrote to Edward Everett, the American Minister at London, a conciliatory letter, phrased doubtless in designed contrast to the correspondence of Palmerston, inviting the United States to join what he called "in truth a holy alliance." At the same time Aberdeen informed Everett that he would send a special minister to the United States to effect a settlement of all points at issue between the two countries. "In the choice of the individual for the mission," the Foreign Secretary had been "mainly influenced by the desire to select a person who would be peculiarly acceptable to the United States as well as eminently qualified for the trust." So in April, 1842, Alexander Baring, Lord Ashburton, arrived at Washington. A long and steadfast friend of America, he was further bound to the country through his wife, a Philadelphia beauty, the daughter of William Bingham, who had sat in the Continental Congress and had been a Senator from Pennsylvania.

One of the early experiences of Ashburton in

Washington was also one of the most singular. The distrust of England that Palmerston with his bullying policy had sown, Aberdeen and Ashburton now had to reap. Not only the United States but Texas mistrusted the underlying purpose of Great Britain. As a matter of fact, Palmerston had made overtures to Mexico advising the recognition of Texas; but there were persistent rumors — in the words of the Texan representative at Washington — "that Great Britain was furnishing money and supplies to Mexico for the subjugation of Texas." To get at the truth James Reily, at that time the Texan chargé, turned to Clay, a Whig like Webster but temperamentally more open to approach. At Reily's request Clay sought an interview with Ashburton and asked him for a plain statement of England's intentions. In reply he received unconditional assurance, subsequently confirmed by Aberdeen, that England would never interfere in favor of Mexico.

Meanwhile Texas had at last dispatched a minister to England, Ashbel Smith, by whom the formal ratifications of the British-Texan treaties were presented. But in Mexico discontent broke out again. This new development was due to the explosions in the American newspapers over the capture of

San Antonio in March, 1842. Waddy Thompson, the newly arrived United States minister to Mexico, encountered bitter complaints in Mexico City to the effect that in all parts of the United States "no voice was heard but that of war with Mexico and of aid to Texas." At the end of May Bocenegra, the Mexican Minister of Foreign Relations, sent a circular note to the resident diplomatic corps denouncing American "violations" of neutrality and virtually intimating war. His reasoning was precisely that with which Americans became indignantly familiar seventy-five years later. Thompson replied with the same invocation of common sense and international law which was afterward and in almost the same connection addressed to the no less obdurate Germans. The freedom of speech tolerated both in the United States and in England forbade government interference with public meetings. Ample illustrations of this freedom of speech were at hand. Almost coincident with a pro-Texas meeting at New Orleans which had given great offense in Mexico, there was held in the same city a meeting in favor of repealing the Irish Union; in England, without protests from the United States, meetings were held "denouncing a large portion of our people and our institutions in language in comparison with which that used in public meetings towards Mexico, is the language of compliment."

The discussion continued. Other equally offensive notes which Bocenegra issued drew from Webster a stern reply. In July he wrote to Thompson: "You will write a note to M. de Bocenegra, in which you will say . . . that the President of the United States considers the language and tone of that letter derogatory to the character of the United States and highly offensive . . . that the conduct of the United States in regard to the war between Mexico and Texas, having been always hitherto governed by a strict and impartial regard to its neutral obligations, will not be changed or altered in any respect or in any degree. If for this, the Government of Mexico shall see fit to change the relations existing between the two countries, the responsibility remains with herself."

It was while both Bocenegra and Webster were thus threatening war that Texas made an ill-judged move. Relying on the friendly attitude of Aberdeen toward the United States, the Government of Texas instructed its minister, Ashbel Smith, to ask whether England and France would not join with the United States in a "triple interposition" between Texas and Mexico. Apparently Houston and his advisers did not understand the true attitudes of the neutral powers and their fixed resolve in 1842 not to be drawn into the Mexican War, unless it might be in their own quarrels. Guizot, the Minister of Louis Philippe, gave the matter a polite hearing but pointed out that the strained relations between Mexico and the United States made the scheme a very doubtful one. Aberdeen, bent entirely upon conciliatory policies, was more outspoken, frankly disapproved the scheme, and thought that each power could use its good offices to more advantage if independent of the others. Thus the proposed triple interposition came to nothing.

Aberdeen was genuinely desirous, however, for peace between Texas and Mexico. Immediately upon the recognition of Texas he had instructed the British Minister in Mexico to put the case as forcibly as possible before the Mexican Government. He argued that it was impossible for Mexico ever to reconquer Texas and that it was in Mexico's interest to create a buffer state between herself and the United States. He pointed out that were a Mexican conquest of Texas possible, the United States would doubtless frustrate it by annexing Texas.   Finally, he suggested that the Mexicans "should not allow themselves to suppose that they can at any time count on succour from Great Britain in their struggles with Texas, or with the United States.   Great Britain is determined to remain strictly neutral."   So unpromising had been Santa Anna's reception of these overtures on the part of Great Britain that the matter was dropped.

Then came the flare-up of the war in the autumn of 1842 with Woll's invasion in September and his raiding of San Antonio.   In October occurred Jones's fiasco at Monterey, which incensed the Mexicans.   In December the surrender at Mier took place.   Early in 1843 the Mier prisoners were massacred.   But just when the outlook for Texas was very dark things began to mend and Aberdeen saw another opportunity to play the mediator.

Among the prisoners carried off by Woll from San Antonio was James W. Robinson, once Lieutenant Governor of Texas.   In the terrible days when the Mier prisoners were wandering in the mountains or starving to death, Robinson was shut up in the castle of Perote.   Thence he wrote to Santa Anna saying that Texas was tired of the war and that he was sure he could negotiate a reunion with Mexico.   Santa Anna, remembering his own

9

strategy after San Jacinto, was not quite taken in but appears to have reasoned that one prisoner more or less did not matter, and that he might as well take the risk. He therefore released Robinson, giving him a signed statement of his terms of peace. From the Mexican point of view these terms contained a real concession: if Texas would acknowledge the sovereignty of Mexico, the Texan Government should be granted so large a measure of autonomy as to make it independent in all but name.

In April, 1843, Robinson laid these terms before President Houston. By this time the British Minister in Texas, Captain Charles Elliot, R. N., was deep in the confidence of Houston — or thought he was. The object of Houston's diplomatic conduct can only be conjectured. That he took different attitudes at different times toward England and toward America is established, but his intentions are still a matter of debate. Did he pass through genuine changes in point of view or was he, as some will have it, always playing one game under several disguises? Was he, when he posed as a lover of England in the period that now begins, really championing Texan independence, or was he scheming to frighten the United States into offering annexation? These questions remain as yet unanswered. What we do know is that in 1843 Houston appeared to turn away from the American affiliation and certainly began to lean heavily on the friendship of England. At his request Elliot, through the British Minister at Mexico City, arranged an armistice. Houston by proclamation suspended hostilities. As might have been expected, nothing came of the ensuing negotiations. Texas would not acknowledge Mexican sovereignty. Mexico would not recognize Texan independence. For more than a year, however, the miserable Mexican War was suspended.

It was in May, 1843, that Santa Anna's terms of peace with Texas, carried by the released prisoner Robinson, were communicated to Aberdeen. He thought they were not of "a very practical description." Nevertheless he wrote to Elliot to make every effort to persuade Texas that virtual independence was worth the "nominal concession" demanded by Santa Anna. What he probably thought and what all shrewd observers must have thought was that both Texas and Mexico were for the moment exhausted and that each was playing for time in which to recuperate.

Aberdeen, true to his conciliatory impulse, would have liked to use this pause in the war to effect a permanent peace. In the early summer of 1843 his career as Foreign Secretary was as yet distinctly bright. The difficult task of undoing the bad effect upon America of Palmerston's diplomacy appeared to have been accomplished. The Ashburton mission had ended brilliantly in a treaty concluded at Washington in August, 1842. If the Oregon question was still open, at least the other vexatious matters concerning the Maine boundary and the slave trade were settled. The provisions of the Quintuple Treaty were virtually extended to the United States. The complex American problem had thus been reduced to the two questions of Oregon and Texas. To both of these Aberdeen was giving careful thought in the early summer of 1843.

Other considerations besides rounding out his foreign policy were pressing Aberdeen toward a more active course with regard to Texas. British bondholders clamored for a policy that would give Mexico peace, prosperity, and a chance to pay its debts. Moreover, the British cotton trade was just then in a state of depression.[1] Undoubtedly

[1] Certain recent historians have made much, perhaps too much, of this business depression. Aberdeen, subsequent to the summer of 1843, is regarded by some scholars as a diplomatic ogre seeking to devour the world in the interests of British business. We may dismiss this extreme view. There is no denying that during a part

Aberdeen wanted to see Texas, Mexico, and the United States, all at peace, all prosperous, all with the best of feeling toward England. Incidentally he may have thought it would be beneficial to England if there were another great cotton field in the world, one whose rulers inclined toward free trade. Texas, if securely independent, would be such a field. He believed that the Texans wanted independence, and Houston diligently encouraged this view. What Aberdeen did next, from the strictly diplomatic point of view, was undoubtedly a blunder, but he was under an illusion with regard to the real desire of the Texans, and did not realize how deeply his relation to America had been changed by Webster's retirement from the State Department a few months before. The new policy was intimately connected with the anti-slavery agitation in England. Three important steps had been taken for the suppression of the slave trade.

The three international agreements — the Quintuple Treaty, the Texan Treaty, the Webster-Ashburton Treaty — were all fresh in the public

---

of his career his motives are obscure. But that period does not date from 1843. It is safest to take his actions during that year at their face value. Especially it is well to give heed to his own statements of his motives. While not at all a great man, neither was he an evil one.

mind and seemed to mark an era. Abolitionists everywhere took heart, thinking their day was at hand. Ashbel Smith as early as January, 1843, was aware of the working of this powerful force and, thinking he perceived a reaction to it on the part of the British Ministry, he wrote home:

It is the purpose of some persons in England to procure the abolition of slavery in Texas. They propose to accomplish this end by friendly negotiation and by the concession of what will be deemed equivalents. I believe the equivalents contemplated are a guarantee by Great Britain of the Independence of Texas — discriminating duties in favor of Texian products and perhaps a negotiation of a loan, or some means by which the finances of Texas can be readjusted. . . .

Rely on it, as certain, that in England it is intended to make an effort, and that some things are already in train to accomplish if possible the abolition of slavery in Texas. And might not Texas exhausted as just described, listen in a moment of folly to such overtures of the British Government? . . .

The independence of Texas and the existence of slavery in Texas is a question of life or death to the slave holding states of the American Union. . . . *The establishment of a free state on the territory of Texas is a darling wish of England for which scarcely any price would be regarded as to* [sic] *great. The bargain once struck what remedy remains to the South.*[1]

[1] *Texan Diplomatic Correspondence*, vol. ii, pp. 1105–1106. The italics are in the original.

Ashbel Smith's surmise as to the ultimate aims of the British Ministry must be read in the light of later events. He was not mistaken as to the renewed activity of the abolitionists. Under the auspices of the British and Foreign Anti-Slavery Society a world's convention of opponents of slavery was arranged to meet in London from June 13th to June 20, 1843. As an event in the development of abolition this convention does not at present concern us, but as a political event, it is of the first magnitude.

This world's convention naturally drew to London the most militant American abolitionists. Among them was Stephen Pearl Andrews from Galveston, Texas. Lundy's dream of a Texas filled with anti-slavery colonies, though it had never been realized, had not been entirely vain. There was some — it is very difficult to say how much — anti-slavery sentiment in Texas, and the new ferment of anti-slavery enthusiasm the world over had its effect among the Texan abolitionists. Andrews, as their representative, set out for London. Passing through the United States he joined another militant abolitionist, Lewis Tappan, and together they called on the grim leader of their cause, John Quincy Adams. In his diary Adams has recorded this visit. The passage is worth bracketing with the one already quoted from Ashbel Smith. The entry which Adams made runs thus:

Mr. Tappan had with him the New Orleans Bee of the 15th and 16th May, containing several long articles sounding the trumpet of alarm at the symptoms recently manifested in Texas of a strong party with a fixed design to abolish slavery. . . . Mr. Andrews . . . is now about to embark in the steamer Caledonia, tomorrow, for England, with a view to obtain the aid of the British government to the cause. . . . I bade him God speed, and told him that I believed the freedom of this country and of all mankind depended upon the direct, formal, open and avowed interference of Great Britain to accomplish the abolition of slavery in Texas; but that I distrusted the sincerity of the present British administration in the anti-slavery cause.

The Convention in London in the month of June was, of course, a great event and it was watched by all sorts of people, from all sorts of points of view — by such political enemies as Lord Aberdeen and Lord Brougham; by the keen and observant envoy from Texas; above all, by a singular American busybody, Duff Green, whose importance will presently appear.

A committee of the Convention, sometimes referred to as "the Tappan Committee," obtained an audience with Aberdeen which proved to be an historic event. Precisely what took place during this interview is somewhat doubtful. The committee gave one version; Lord Aberdeen, another. Doubtless it was an instance of hot-headed enthusiasts misunderstanding the very cautious statements of one who sympathized with them personally but had not at the moment any intention of committing himself officially. What the committee believed Aberdeen to have said gave rise to the report, destined to have wide influence in America, that England would guarantee the interest of a Texan loan if its proceeds should be applied to the purchase and emancipation of slaves.

Aberdeen's version of the conference — which was not known in the United States until the Committee's version had become a fixed tradition accepted by such incompatibles as Calhoun and Adams — was expressed in reply to a direct inquiry from Smith, in whom the version circulated by the committee roused alarm.

His Lordship replied in effect [Smith wrote] that it is the well known policy and wish of the British Government to abolish slavery everywhere; that its abolition in Texas is deemed very desirable and he spoke to this point at some length, as connected with British policy and British interests and in reference to the United States. He added, that there was no disposition on the part of the British Government to interfere improperly on this subject, and that they would not give the Texian government cause to complain; he was not prepared to say whether the British Government would consent hereafter to make such compensation to Texas as would enable the slaveholders to abolish slavery, the object is deemed so important perhaps they might, though he could not say certainly. . . .

Lord Aberdeen also stated that despatches had been recently sent to Mr. Doyle, the British Chargé d' Affaires at Mexico, instructing him to renew the tender of British mediation based on the abolition of slavery in Texas, and declaring that abolition would be a *great moral triumph for Mexico*. Your Department will not fail to remark that this despatch to Mr. Doyle appears to introduce a new and important condition into "mediation." . . .

The British Government greatly desire the abolition of slavery in Texas as a part of their general policy in reference to their colonial and commercial interests and mainly in reference to its future influence on slavery in the United States.

Here we find Aberdeen's new policy. Mexico was to be persuaded to abandon the demand for a nominal sovereignty over Texas and was to concede independence; the *quid pro quo* was to be the "moral triumph" of a Texan assent to abolition; as Aberdeen told Smith, this programme had already been communicated to Doyle in Mexico. Soon after this interview Aberdeen wrote again to Doyle reviewing his interview with the "Tappan Committee," repeating his desire to have Texas "confer entire emancipation on all persons within its territory," and concluding with the statement that "H. M. Government desires that you should press this point earnestly on the attention of the Mexican Government." That Aberdeen should have supposed Santa Anna and his gangsters susceptible to the charms of what the Englishman considered a "moral triumph" is strange beyond expression. But apparently Aberdeen was sincere in this belief. And he seems not to have had the slightest suspicion how his course would be interpreted by the successors of Webster at Washington. It now remains to be seen how this conciliatory Lord Aberdeen, a statesman following the will-o'-the-wisp of his political illusions, had digged for himself a great pitfall.

CHAPTER VIII

IN this period of American life, distrust of England was broadcast. The dominant men in politics were of the generation succeeding the Revolution, and the impression of their youth — of the bitter hostility to Great Britain in 1812 — remained with them to color their views and shape their conduct. Men like Calhoun and John Quincy Adams, who had little else in common except their ability, were at one in their reading of some ulterior motive into every British act. It is the pathetic fallacy of the time that so few American patriots could see beyond their immediate horizon. Calhoun interpreted a certain set of facts as evidence that England desired the extinction of slavery, and perhaps even the dissolution of the Union, in her own commercial interest, while Adams reasoned from the same set of facts that England's "interest is to sustain and cherish slavery."

The statesman who was now Secretary of State, had the limitations of his day.   Abel P. Upshur based his foreign policy on the belief that England was aiming to abolish "domestic slavery throughout the continent and islands of America in order to find or create new markets for the products of her home industry, and at the same time destroy all competition with the industry of her colonies." In accounting for Upshur's foreign policy it must be remembered also that his point of view was exclusively American, the point of view of a "practical" man with a clear, though narrow, vision of cause and effect, and of a slaveholder and a believer in slavery.

About the time that Upshur became Secretary, Duff Green began writing home sensational accounts of the relations between Aberdeen and the Tappan Committee.   He wrote to Calhoun, who passed his letters on to Upshur, and also directly to Upshur.   As Green was a politician of some prominence, a newspaper editor, and a faithful Democrat, and as he had met in Europe some distinguished people and had been invited by Delane to write articles for *The Times* on American conditions, his reports on Aberdeen struck his American friends with the force of oracles.   Two misapprehensions of Aberdeen which Green circulated alarmed Upshur. One of them was the account given out by the Tappan Committee of their interview with the Foreign Secretary, according to which Aberdeen promised to guarantee an Anglo-Texan emancipation loan. He expressed his other misapprehension when he said "that the British Government deem it so important to prevent the annexation of Texas to the United States that they were disposed to support the loan if it should be required to prevent annexation." Thus Upshur and Calhoun formed a conception of Aberdeen's foreign policy which they never abandoned.

The Anti-slavery Convention and the incident of the Tappan Committee were widely reported throughout the United States. Anti-slavery people were jubilant, slaveholders alarmed. The prospect of a free Texas offering an asylum to runaway slaves — a second Canada only a river's width away — stirred the slaveowning oligarchy of the South into action. Though defeated in 1838 and put aside, as it seemed, by the Whig victory in the election of 1840, annexation might now have another chance. Tyler had broken with the Whigs who had elected him. In Upshur he had put at the head of his cabinet an avowed annexationist. The indiscretion attributed to Aberdeen was just what was needed to breathe new life into the cause. If anything more was required, it was supplied by a conversation between Aberdeen and Brougham in the House of Lords. Brougham inquired what the Government was doing in Texas; he wanted to know whether Mexico was being pressed to recognize Texas on the basis of emancipation; and he made the diplomatically unfortunate remark that abolition, if it could be effected in Texas, would react against slavery in the United States. Aberdeen refused to explain his course and insisted that it was not the proper time for submitting to Parliament a statement of his Mexican policy, but he assured his noble friend that so far as slavery was concerned his refusal "did not arise from indifference but from quite a contrary reason." A report of this conversation printed in the New York *Herald* on September 20, 1843, drew the conclusion that England was aiming at the destruction of the United States.

These European events, though Upshur assigned to them prime importance in reviving the annexation issue, were not the only matters troubling him in the early autumn of 1843. Though Texas in 1838, after Adams' great victory in Congress, had withdrawn its request for annexation, the request had been renewed in 1842, and remained outstanding till the summer of 1843, when President Houston again withdrew it.

What, in the light of the supposed British intrigues, lay behind this action? Isaac van Zandt, the Texan Minister at Washington, wrote home in September that it had "fired" Upshur with renewed zeal for annexation. Van Zandt perhaps did not make sufficient allowance for the perspective in which the event was placed before Upshur's imagination by the news from London and by the talk of the abolitionists.

As a matter of fact there was nothing mysterious or sinister in Houston's withdrawal of the request for annexation. Had it been known at Washington on the day it was ordered — July 6, 1843 — its significance might have been perceived. Only three weeks had elapsed since Houston's proclamation of June 13, 1843, ordering a cessation of hostilities under the Robinson armistice. What could have been more absurd than to discuss terms which involved a possible recognition of Mexican sovereignty by Texas, while there remained outstanding a formal request for annexation to the United States?

But as the summer progressed and the negotiations with Mexico showed no sign of coming to anything, Houston became nervous and furnished students of history some cause to quarrel over his motives. There is something to be said for simply accepting the record at its face value. During the previous year Houston had received distinct rebuffs from the United States. The Adams manifesto threatening civil war if Texas were annexed was but a few months old. The treaty of commerce and amity between Texas and the United States had been rejected by the American Senate within the year. To be sure, Webster, the great enemy of Texas, was gone from the State Department, but as yet his retirement had not produced a change of front toward Texas. On the other hand, English officials had negotiated the Robinson armistice. For the first time since the war began, Texas had a real breathing space. What more natural than that Houston — who resented the successive rebuffs brought about by Webster and Adams, who was grateful for the respite in the war, and who hoped for some sort of peace — was eager at this moment to be unembarrassed by an American affiliation and to make the most of the friendship of England?

10

When in the late autumn Houston heard from Van Zandt that Upshur had proposed a treaty of annexation, the situation in which he found himself had changed, though it is quite possible that his sympathies at this time were still definitely pro-British. Houston told Charles Elliot "that with the independence of Texas recognized by Mexico, he would never consent to any treaty on this project of annexation to the United States." On the ground of what he said to Upshur some critics have charged him with duplicity, for Van Zandt was to tell Upshur that the matter would be considered only on receipt of a definite proposal from the United States Senate.

The clue to Houston's temporizing is to be found in certain occurrences in Mexico. Three incidents that were hardly noticed at Washington, but that loomed large in Texas occurred in the latter part of 1843. One was no more dignified than a quarrel between Doyle and the Mexican authorities over a British flag exhibited among certain trophies of war. Doyle's demand for the removal of the flag and the squabbling of the Mexicans caused a cessation of diplomatic relations, a popular demonstration against England, and even threats of war. To Houston, who had hoped that England would find a way to permanent peace, this temporary paralyzing of her influence in Mexico was disconcerting. A second disquieting happening was the pacification of Yucatan. Santa Anna had been seriously embarrassed throughout the year by the civil war against his administration in Yucatan, and his consent to the armistice may have come from his desire to center his whole strength upon Yucatan. But toward the end of the year the quarrel was made up. Just when Houston saw his great friend, England, become powerless in Mexico, he also saw his worst enemy, Santa Anna, turn toward Texas, his purpose clearly shown by the third alarming circumstance. Mexico knew that volunteers from the United States had always formed the chief recruiting supply of the Texan army. In 1843 the Mexican Government issued a proclamation announcing that any foreigner who invaded the territory of the republic whether "accompanied by a few or many adventurers" should, if taken with arms in his hands, be shown no quarter but should "be immediately put to death."

Considering the Mexican situation, Houston plainly saw where his line of safety lay. So imperative was his need of an ally that he dared not refuse any offer. It is quite likely that his first choice would have been an independent Texas, and he continued to assure Elliot that he still hoped for it. Nevertheless Houston would not commit himself adversely to the American proposal. He was maneuvering for position and seeking a means of defense against the dreaded Mexican blow.

Meanwhile Upshur at Washington, it would seem, dreaded a blow from outside as much as Houston in Texas. Though Everett at London, by Upshur's instructions, had asked Aberdeen what were his intentions, and though Aberdeen had denied any intention to intervene in Texas, the denial as reported by Everett served if anything to increase Upshur's conviction that England was playing a game of deception with the United States. "The subject of domestic slavery," Everett wrote in his report of the interview, "was never so much as mentioned or alluded to by the British Minister to the Government of Texas, except to disclaim in most emphatic terms any intention on the part of England to interfere with it here. Her Texas policy was to build up a power independent of the United States who could raise cotton enough to supply the World; of which power slavery would be a necessary element."

Whether or no Aberdeen was candid in this interview may be left to his biographers. To Upshur, at least, the whole truth seemed to lie in Everett's conclusion that England desired an independent Texas as rival to the United States in the growing of cotton. He was confirmed in his belief that England was an ogre seeking her commercial interests utterly without scruple. To defeat the British move against Texas was, therefore, for the United States a matter of life or death. From this time forward the great majority of the anti-British sank all other considerations before their overpowering fear of the ogre in London. Subsequently Calhoun asserted this fact in so many words and insisted that it was not for sectional but for national reasons that he urged the annexation of Texas. At the time his enemies did not believe him. Certain later historians have sought to prove him insincere by exposing the misapprehension on which his reasoning was based; but such a refutation concerns his political acumen and not his motive. It becomes increasingly plain that both Calhoun and Upshur, carried away by their traditional dread of Great Britain, saw the Texas question as a matter of international strategy.

Believing the American danger to be real and

acute, Upshur was set on edge by Houston's equivocal attitude during the latter part of 1843. Van Zandt, also provoked, exceeded his authority and negotiated a treaty of annexation. Then, perhaps alarmed at his own temerity and on second thought appreciating Houston's position better, he demanded a guarantee of protection by the United States against Mexico in the course of negotiation, should Texas consent to negotiate. Here was the crux of the Texan issue narrowly considered. Should the United States enter the war? We have seen that a few years earlier almost all Americans, even friends of Texas like Preston, were resolute not to annex a war; but at that time the British ogre had not been raised from the dead. Its resurrection now transformed the case. Convinced that England was moving upon Texas and that she must be kept out at all cost, Upshur prepared for war with Mexico. Verbal assurance was given Van Zandt that Texas would be defended against Mexico. At the same time Upshur sent a virtual ultimatum to Houston in which he very nearly threatened to go over Houston's head and appeal direct to the Texan people. Upshur further stated that annexation could now be carried in the United States Senate, warned Houston against trusting the friendship of England, and cited the fable of the wolf and the lamb.

It is highly probable that Van Zandt, not being in sympathy with Houston, had anticipated Upshur's implied threat and was already corresponding with the Department of State, behind Houston's back. At least it is certain that a popular movement for annexation was started in Texas at the close of 1843. From this Houston held off, thereby provoking sharp criticism. He was accused of acting too often behind a "veil of secrecy." Presently, being pushed forward by Washington and by the clamor at home, he laid the whole situation before the Texan Congress and emphasized the great danger, should negotiations with the United States fail, that England and France might take offense at such disregard of their good offices and leave Texas alone to face a vengeful Mexico. He insisted upon at least a defensive alliance with the United States before entering upon negotiations. The possibility of such an alliance seemed to be established shortly afterwards by the receipt of Van Zandt's dispatch reporting the verbal assurance of protection. To clinch the matter Houston applied to the American minister William S. Murphy, who stated in writing to the Texan

Government that "neither Mexico nor any other power will be permitted to invade Texas on account of any negotiation" with the United States. This assurance determined Houston, and the next day he sent off a special envoy to coöperate with Van Zandt. On the day following he wrote to his old friend Jackson urging him to use his influence on behalf of annexation, saying that Texas approached the United States "like a bride adorned for her espousal" but intimating that there were other lovers in the field should the presumptive bridegroom prove too coy.

Meanwhile, though the negotiations had been kept secret, the Mexican Minister at Washington scented danger. This official was none other than that same Almonte who, years before, had filled Lundy with erroneous views upon Texas and who now again becomes associated with John Quincy Adams. In December, 1843, Almonte unbosomed himself to Adams and was assured that an annexation treaty could not pass the Senate. Not wholly satisfied, Almonte then interviewed Upshur. The Secretary of State made no secret of his fear that England was striving to control Texas and to injure the United States. Upshur expressed his dread of England by saying that "he would infinitely prefer to see Texas again in possession of the Mexicans than under the influence of the British Government. . . ." When Almonte suggested that England might object to the "sale" of Texas, even if Mexico were willing, Upshur replied that in such an event the United States would go the length of war with England. Almonte's last word was to the effect that before he could again communicate with his Government, Mexican armies would be in the heart of Texas. Before anything further could be done, Upshur was killed by the explosion of a great cannon during an artillery display on the warship *Princeton* on February 28, 1844.

Calhoun now became Secretary of State and no one could have been found more likely to continue an anti-British policy. With characteristic boldness he sent for Almonte, informed him that a treaty of annexation was in preparation, and asked whether Mexico could be induced to consent. Almonte replied that annexation meant war and that he would ask for his passports the moment the treaty was ratified. With the issue thus clearly defined, the diplomats parted.

Nothing daunted, Calhoun turned to the Texan representatives — for the special envoy had now arrived — and confirmed the promise of protection. "Should the exigency arise to which you refer in your note to Mr. Upshur," he said in writing to Van Zandt, "I am further directed by the President to say, that, during the pendency of the treaty of annexation, he would deem it his duty to use all the means placed within his power by the constitution to protect Texas from all foreign invasion." On April 12, 1844, the Texan envoy signed the treaty of annexation.

In the six weeks since Upshur's death the Mexican Minister on his part had labored industriously. The letters which he sent to his Government during March told of conferences with congressmen, senators, and other persons of importance; he was assured that New England, New York, and Pennsylvania would secede rather than permit annexation; the abolitionists would all stand by Mexico. He therefore concluded that it was most important to invade Texas without delay. The one discouraging circumstance was the attitude of the British Minister, who gave no hope that England would try to prevent annexation by force. Almonte was accordingly convinced that England's great trade with the United States would prevent war.

Plainly Washington was a boiling pot when the

treaty was signed. It is highly probable that the Administration had become doubtful of its strength. Perhaps for this reason it delayed ten days before sending the treaty to the Senate; or perhaps it sought to arouse public interest. The political strategy of these ten days is not altogether clear, but the new Secretary of State undoubtedly created enemies for the treaty by making public a significant letter to Lord Aberdeen.

Among Upshur's unfinished business Calhoun had found a letter from Pakenham, the British Minister, enclosing a dispatch from Aberdeen. Reports from America of the great excitement over his dealings with the Tappan Committee had at last come to Aberdeen's ears, and he saw that the American excitement must immediately be quieted. With that end in view he sent the dispatch now known as the first paper in the Calhoun-Pakenham correspondence. This letter was little more than a plain statement of Aberdeen's attitude toward Texas, repeating practically what he had said to Ashbel Smith the previous summer. He denied that he had any secret design with regard to Texas and frankly admitted his desire for abolition "throughout the world" but insisted that England would do nothing "secretly or underhand."

He said further that England's interests in Texas were purely commercial and that she had "no thought or intention of seeking to act directly or indirectly in a political sense on the United States through Texas."

To this letter Calhoun wrote a long reply, a copy of which was submitted to the Senate with the treaty. There can be no doubt that in his own mind it was an argument for Americanism, an appeal to his countrymen to resent a foreign interference with a domestic institution. His text was Aberdeen's avowal of his desire to see slavery abolished throughout the world. From this Calhoun drew the conclusion that England desired a world unsafe for slavery; and from that it followed that she would enforce her views on the United States by violence. Would any American, slaveholder or other, stand by and see his country's institutions mutilated by an invader? Such was the sentiment Calhoun wished to inspire in every American. Unfortunately for his cause, he did not confine himself to the general theme but discussed at length the merits of slavery and compared the conditions of negroes in the South and in the North. The precise effect of this letter has never been determined. Did it defeat the treaty? Did it fall flat?

Who knows! It aroused a storm of protest and the treaty was eventually rejected by the Senate, but whether these facts are causally related is not easily told.

The Texan annexation treaty was before the Senate from April until June. During that time the national conventions were held, that of the Whigs on the 1st of May and that of the Democrats later in the same month. The Whig platform did not mention Texas. Clay, the foregone conclusion in the way of Whig candidate, had previously issued a letter defining his position with regard to Texas. In this document Clay held that it was "perfectly idle and ridiculous, if not dishonorable, to talk of resuming our title to Texas," insisted that annexation meant war with Mexico, opposed the project, and poohpoohed the idea that England was moving against the United States through Texas.

Among the Democrats the annexation issue produced a complicated intrigue, the details of which are not important here. It is enough to say that Van Buren, until then the most promising candidate for nomination, spoiled his chances by a letter. With his eye on the political situation in the North and fearful of losing the anti-slavery wing of his party, which was now large, Van Buren came out frankly against annexation on the ground that it meant war with Mexico. In contrast to this attitude, James K. Polk took up Clay's challenge and in unequivocal terms announced himself "in favor of immediate re-annexation of Texas," and the Democratic politicians, who saw that at this moment they needed a fighting man, nominated Polk.

As the Presidential campaign began, the foreign affairs of the United States entered upon a new and very singular chapter. In both connections Clay held the center of the stage. His great personality, so hypnotic in its effect upon his associates, was also to impress Aberdeen and to give direction to his policy. As far back as December, 1843, Clay had met Elliot, then on a visit to New Orleans, and had assured him that he need not be alarmed over rumors of projected annexation, for no annexation treaty would pass the Senate. These assurances Elliot sent to Aberdeen. Later on, Pakenham told Aberdeen that he could rely on "the whole strength of Mr. Clay's party" being thrown against annexation.

There seems little doubt that the Whigs at this time appeared to Aberdeen as the dominant American party. How completely he was convinced that

his best course lay in close coöperation with them,
is shown by a passage in a subsequent dispatch to
France in which he confessed alarm lest his policy
had been "throwing additional weight into the
scale of . . . Mr. Polk . . . and proportionately
diminishing Mr. Clay's Election to the Presidential Chair." Until very recently Aberdeen's part
in this year of destiny, 1844, has been ignored by
American historians. Even today his motives are
uncertain and his actions seem in part ambiguous.
Three illusions in his mind furnish a clue to his
policy: first, that he had the dominant American
party on his side; second, that opposition to annexation represented only the alarm of slaveholders
over the question of abolition in Texas; and, third,
that Texas was opposed to annexation and would
regard as an act of aggression any attempt by the
United States to achieve it. The different chapters in Aberdeen's diplomacy may be marked off, as
first one and then another of his political illusions
faded away.

The most important of these — the vision of a
troubled Texas, afraid of both Mexico and the
United States, and eager to be independent of
both — was inspired by a letter from Elliot, reporting that Houston assured him his demands for

protection by the United States were intended as an impossible condition which would bring annexation to a standstill. He hoped that Great Britain would "find means of preventing all further risk of complication in that direction." During most of 1844 Aberdeen was in two minds towards the United States. On the one hand, Upshur's anti-British agitation incensed him. Tyler's message of December, 1843, contained sneers at England that caused Aberdeen to lose his temper. He wrote Pakenham "to state to Mr. Upshur H. M.'s Govt. would have been glad if they could have discovered in the Message greater evidence of that disinterested policy, the presumed absence of which in other quarters, the President has thought necessary to call to the Notice of his Countrymen." Pakenham wisely disobeyed instructions and did not deliver this communication. Aberdeen's temper after Calhoun's reply to Pakenham was foreseen by the Minister when he wrote home: "Your Lordship will perceive with surprise and displeasure . . . that the explanations furnished by Her Majesty's Government have been received in a sense quite contrary to their obvious and literal meaning." Plenty of cause here for temper!

The Oregon negotiation was, however, still

JAMES K. POLK

Daguerreotype.   In the collection of L. C. Handy, Washington.

JAMES K. POLK

Daguerreotype.   In the collection of L. C. Handy, Washington.

outstanding, and Aberdeen was eager to bring it to a happy conclusion. During half the year his course vacillated between an indulgence of his temper and a consideration of his best interests. In his calmer moments he could not forget the watchful attitude of British business, with its enormous American trade, and at such times he must have fully realized that a breach with the United States would have wrecked the ministry. Behind Aberdeen stood Peel, the Prime Minister, an incomparably larger man and one who kept a far better balance between his impulses and his actions. On both of these men the opposition in Parliament served a warning in May when it demanded what the Government was doing in America, basing the inquiry on a suspicion that it was meddling with the internal affairs of other countries. Both Aberdeen and Peel refused to commit themselves. Shortly before, the Liverpool *Mercury* had declared that a war with the United States, even if successful, would so damage British trade as to be a "calamity of the most fatal description."

Against this complex background must be seen Aberdeen's rash move earlier in the year when he invited France to join with him in a protest against the pending treaty. Guizot, always agreeably disposed towards the British authorities, instructed the French Minister at Washington to coöperate with Pakenham. Fortunately for Aberdeen the two ministers agreed that Aberdeen's plan, if carried out, would not play into Clay's hands but into those of his enemies, would stimulate the anti-British feeling, and would give annexation a trump card. The protest, it seems, was not made.

During the month of May, when the treaty was before the Senate and Clay was forcing the issue with an apparent firmness destined soon to disappear, Aberdeen resolved to get entirely free of his entanglement with the international abolition of slavery. This he did before the month was over by entering into new negotiations with Mexico in which he definitely withdrew all his previous suggestions as to abolition in Texas. Three days later he sent a dispatch to Pakenham informing him of this change of front, accompanied by a full statement of the attitude of the British Government on the subject of slavery in the United States. Therein he repeated his condemnation of slavery but promised to refrain carefully from any steps which could affect the interest of the United States "in this particular."

If Aberdeen's view of the American situation

had been correct, if Clay had dominated it, and if the militant slavery faction had been his only serious enemies, Aberdeen might well have congratulated himself on a shrewd stroke. Doubtless he thought he had the situation in hand when, in this new overture to Mexico, he proposed on the one hand that Mexico should acknowledge Texan independence and on the other that Texas should pledge herself not to consent to annexation by any other power, and that England and France should guarantee the pledge.

A short but obscure chapter in Aberdeen's diplomacy thus begins. While awaiting action by Mexico, he obtained the assent of the amiable Guizot to his new plan. Then with apparent abruptness Aberdeen changed front once more. On the 18th of July, before any reply to his overture had been received from Mexico, he wrote to the British Ambassador at Paris that the scheme must be abandoned or at least indefinitely postponed. What had happened between May and July? What illusion had dissolved?

Clay's firm opposition to annexation was based on his belief that it was safe policy. The illusion he had helped create in Aberdeen dominated him as well in that month of May, when he thought he would certainly be the next President of the United States. At first it looked as if, in forcing the fight, he had split the Democrats. When the treaty came to a vote it lacked the necessary two-thirds majority. The seven Democrats who voted against it were taking revenge for the Van Buren faction because the party machine had not accepted their favorite. It was quickly made plain, however, that this was a case of the sulks and not a settled policy. Thomas H. Benton, chief supporter of Van Buren, first voted against the treaty and then came out in favor of annexation through the action of Congress. All factions of the Democratic party accepted annexation as their cardinal doctrine. Van Buren himself offered no opposition, and his personal following in New York, which was the "pivotal State," took their strategic place in the battle.

Each week of the campaign made it clearer that Clay and Aberdeen, with their illusion that the militant slaveholders formed the whole strength of the annexation movement, had made a fatal blunder. The United States wanted Texas. At any rate, so loud and insistent and widespread was the cry for annexation that Clay, whose ear was to the ground, became alarmed. He began to make admissions, to explain away his position, to prepare to straddle the issue.   At length he wrote the famous letter that killed him politically.   The advocates of annexation had gone too far in defiance of him to swing around like a dog to a whistle because he now offered to accept their terms. When he announced that he would be glad to see Texas annexed if it could be done "without dishonor, without war, upon the common consent of the Union, upon just and fair terms," he shattered the anti-Texas faction.   Whether it could have won if its leader had stuck to his colors is a subject of dispute to this day.

All these moves in the political game were described by Pakenham to Aberdeen.   Both Pakenham and the French Minister perceived the turning of the tide.   A victorious anti-Texas party that would welcome or at least acquiesce in the Anglo-French guarantee of Texan independence proved to be a dream.   Both ministers warned their Governments not to proceed with the plan.   The determining letter appears to be the dispatch to Pakenham dated the 27th of June.   Though at that date Clay had not yet written the letter that destroyed him, Pakenham's political insight read the situation correctly.   While still hoping much from Clay's election, he made the remarkable prophecy that, even if elected, Clay would not after all be able to stop annexation, but merely to secure for it a fair consideration. Pakenham told Aberdeen almost in so many words that, if England and France should pursue their plan "without the consent and concurrence of this country previously obtained," the result might be war. There had arisen "a crisis of the utmost delicacy in our relations with this Country." Other information with regard to the American situation had also come to Aberdeen. Side by side with the Texas question the Oregon question had grown more and more momentous. The Democratic platform declared that the title of the United States to "the whole of the territory of Oregon is clear and unquestionable; that no portion of the same ought to be ceded to England." The whole country rang with the cry: "Fifty-four forty or fight!"

What was the British Ministry to do? The whole thought of Aberdeen upon American affairs during June and July, 1844, has never been disclosed. But the result of his thinking was soon made manifest. There are those who believe that for a brief space his temper overmastered his true interests and that he contemplated war. If that is so, it was indeed a midsummer madness that quickly passed. In late July, Aberdeen was corresponding with Paris and decently burying his ambitious scheme of the previous May. He had decided finally upon an amicable policy towards the United States. As to Texas, the future was to be left to circumstance. Oregon was to be the immediate witness to the desire of Great Britain to settle her American problems in a friendly way. Pakenham pressed Calhoun, who was still at the State Department, to resume negotiations. In August when the American crisis had taken on another and very startling aspect, these two able men, in a tone that was like a cool breeze amid the hot fury of American politics, opened the final chapter in the long controversy over Oregon.

CHAPTER IX

THE DOMESTIC CRISIS OF 1844

WHILE the ostentatious Polk and the unstable Clay imagined they were the great players in the presidential game, the real contest in 1844 lay between Calhoun and another powerful personality, Robert Barnwell Rhett; and that contest was fought out in South Carolina. The fundamental issue between Calhoun and Rhett was not annexation but secession.

We have Rhett's word that he became a secessionist in 1844, and that he was the only one in Congress during that year. He was then a representative from South Carolina. A perfectly fearless and a wonderfully direct man, he had often before then threatened to accept secession as a solution of the sectional conflict. As early as 1838, in a counterblast to a petition against slavery in the District of Columbia, he moved that "the constitution of the United States having proved inadequate to protect the Southern States in the peaceable enjoyment of their rights and property: *Resolved*, that a committee of two members from each State in the Union be appointed to report upon the expediency and practicality of amending the constitution or the best mode of dissolving the Union." He had taken part in those great parliamentary battles in which Adams had led the assaults upon the friends of Texas, and he made his irrevocable decision soon after Adams had threatened a secession of Northern States.

About this time occurred a schism in the Methodist Church which appears to have made a deep impression on the Southern imagination. The Charleston *Mercury*, the newspaper that was Rhett's especial organ, remarked that "the split of the Methodist Church [into the Northern and Southern Churches] is of peculiar significance as marking an epoch — the first dissolution of the Union." Putting all these signs together, Rhett concluded that the experiment of union was a failure. He therefore determined to take Adams at his word and to anticipate his threatened Northern secession by an attempt, at least, to lead the South into secession. Rhett first urged the Southern members of Congress to issue an address to their constituents advocating a convention of the whole South to deal with the Texan question. When this failed, he advanced to the position which he held ever after and which put him fundamentally at odds with Calhoun.   Since the South would not act as a whole, Rhett urged upon the South Carolina delegation that they send home a circular advocating separate action by their own State.   His theory was that if South Carolina seceded the other Southern States would be forced by the instinct of self-preservation to follow her example.   If we may accept the bitter version of this incident recorded in the diary of Governor Hammond, though the plan promised success for a while, "at the eleventh hour Calhoun came in and broke it up chanting praises to the Union and peace."   Rhett thereupon went home, leaving behind him the war-cry, "Texas, with or without the Union."

Partisans of Rhett in South Carolina were already making active demonstrations in favor of annexation.   They held meetings and adopted resolutions.   Though most of these gatherings were not in favor of disunion before Rhett returned upon the ground, some of them were.   For instance, one meeting at Barnwell resolved that if annexation failed "a dissolution of the Union would be both inevitable and highly desirable," and another at Beaufort resolved that, "We will dissolve the Union rather than abandon Texas."

Even before Rhett took command of his forces in person, the movement for secession was progressing so rapidly that in the middle of June the Charleston *Courier*, an anti-Rhett paper, published a letter from "A Plain Man" advising "Mr. Calhoun to send a missionary into the State, for the purpose of attending all political meetings and checking the recklessness and headlong course of his political friends. With great propriety may he exclaim, 'deliver me from my (foolish) friends,' etc."

In the first weeks of the presidential campaign, many South Carolinians were averse to Polk. There was much talk of supporting Tyler for President. There was also much talk of disunion. To combat both these tendencies the *Courier* reiterated quotations of the views of Calhoun and insisted that he and his friends were entirely satisfied with the nomination of Polk. The *Courier* rejoiced "that the disunion spirit, lately revived and thus manifest among us," had not made headway outside the State and held it "a matter of real gratulation that Mr. Calhoun should throw the weight of his great

name against intemperate action of any kind."
The *Mercury* sharply took the *Courier* to task for
its attitude, and the Calhoun organ replied: "We
repeat here our high gratification at the stand
now taken by Mr. Calhoun against separate State
action, or separate Southern action, on matters
of national concernment — we know of no leader
under whom we would more willingly enlist than
our great Southern statesman, should he indeed
return to his first love, recover his nationality of
feeling and unfurl the glorious banner of Union
and Liberty."

Thus the issue was joined. To Calhoun's argument that nothing ought to be done until the election should determine whether Polk or Clay was to
direct events, Rhett had his reply. To his mind it
was no longer a question of the Presidency but of
the House of Representatives. There, more and
more clearly, lay the heart of the problem, as the
House tended to divide on sectional lines. Before
long a solid majority from the free States would
control it. Secession or submission were the al-
ternatives before the South. Since a choice must
be made, why not at once before the enemy forces
had time to consolidate fully?

Rhett took immediate command of his battle in

an address which he delivered on the 31st of July at Bluffton at a public dinner given in his honor. The significant toast was "Disunion the only remedy"; and another toast was "John C. Calhoun — we will follow him as long as he is true to us." The event of the day was, of course, Rhett's speech, in which he clearly defined his position. He saw no hope from the presidential election; the Democratic party throughout the country could not be relied upon to protect the South; Texas must be acquired; the tariff must be abolished; the one way to preserve Southern institutions was to secede. Rhett's speech was enthusiastically received, and the entire assemblage appeared to be with him. "The spirit of Brutus," said the *Mercury*, "has not passed away but will inspire the people until the State once more is free."

During August and September the battle raged. For a time Rhett seemed to be carrying everything before him. He made numerous speeches. He received great ovations. It seemed that the spell of Calhoun had been broken. "If it be true," said a letter which the *Mercury* displayed as an editorial, "that our old commander has bid adieu to his faithful soldiers, another leader, not as able, nor perhaps as judicious in the council yet as brave and determined in the field, it will be no difficult matter to select."

But those who thought that the old commander had lost his hold had been premature in their judgment. While Calhoun remained at Washington negotiating with Pakenham over Oregon, a few letters from him, the reiteration of his views by his recognized agents, and the arguments of the newspapers that represented him, gradually restored his spell. It was a great victory for sheer prestige. By the end of August the resolutions at public dinners were beginning to regain their old tone of hero-worship for Calhoun. Gradually his argument for no action until after the election became the popular one. Rhett's contention that Congress and not the Presidency was the heart of the matter lost its allurement. In September the *Courier* declared that "Mr. Calhoun has been and is still the guiding star for South Carolina."

That Calhoun feared what might follow disunion only less than he feared the consequences of a consolidation of the Union, every biographer has recognized. But time has shown that consolidation or disruption was inevitable, and it was this alternative which Rhett saw in 1844 and Calhoun failed to see. Must Calhoun's defenders come eventually to the conclusion, then, that in 1844 the older statesman was the inferior strategist?

Two considerations interpose to arrest this conclusion. For one thing, Calhoun had a new vision which Rhett had not — the vision of a United South acting as a unit, in place of the older vision of a Southern group of friendly but separate States. It was this vision which Calhoun handed on to those successors of his who beat Rhett a second time in 1851. Another consideration may have ruled Calhoun's action. There can be little doubt that he was hypnotized by his belief that England would turn aggressor in the Western Hemisphere, were it not for the opposition of the United States. When he said that his Texan policy was national not sectional, he told the strict truth. The best proof is his course in South Carolina, the truly pivotal State. We need not say that he had lost strategic insight, but rather that he was keen enough to pierce through sectional limitations. Assuming his view of British policy, what could have seemed more disastrous in 1844 to America than a division of the Union into two weakened republics to replace a single powerful one? Twenty years later, in a similar situation, the third Napoleon tried to conquer Mexico. A divided republic in 1844 would have given the same opportunity, not to the conciliatory Aberdeen, but to the aggressive and anti-American Palmerston, who, but a few months after Rhett's defeat, became Aberdeen's successor. Whether Calhoun was right or wrong in his view of Aberdeen, what great good fortune for America that he kept a united front in the face of Palmerston when such a prize as Texas might have tempted that grand swashbuckler to follow his natural bent!

CHAPTER X

AN ADVENTURE IN IMPERIALISM

THE Democratic victory in November reunited the party. Taking the election of Polk to be an indorsement of the programme of annexation, the party leaders set confidently to work. What could not be done by treaty, should be done now by action of Congress. A few Whigs, equally obedient to the popular will, joined the friends of Texas. A joint resolution was adopted by both Houses inviting Texas to become a State of the Union and was signed by President Tyler on March 1, 1845. Thereupon Almonte demanded his passports and left Washington.

Meanwhile Mexico had become, to use a modern term, isolated. We may date her isolation from the end of April. Mexico was at that time deeply stirred by a report that annexation was impending. An appeal to the British Minister was met by the assertion that "any assistance from England must be a moral one for that whatever disposition may have at one time existed to go beyond that line had now been withdrawn." Though Aberdeen was led by the Texan Government into one more attempt to intervene in the interest of independence, it was as mediator only that he acted. As a result, Mexico offered to recognize the Republic of Texas if it would remain independent. But Texas was treating also with the United States, with regard to annexation, and when the two proposals — peace with Mexico and independence or no peace and annexation — were laid before a convention that assembled on July 4, 1845, Texas accepted the invitation of the United States.

And now the center of the stage belongs to the new President of the United States, James Knox Polk. Undoubtedly Polk did not want war; but he was as ignorant of the Mexican character as Adams or Jackson and treated the Mexican ultimatum as of no consequence. He regarded the Texan episode as closed — as, with skillful diplomacy, perhaps it might have been — and now maneuvered to bring forward a scheme of his own. His first aim was to restore diplomatic relations with Mexico. During the whole of his first year of office he made tortuous and fruitless attempts to induce the Mexican

Government to eat its words, assume again that there was peace between the nations, and receive an American Minister. But in all these efforts he failed to consider the Mexican point of view and the internal situation with its swift and revolutionary changes of control, and the fact that, in addition to the Government, there was a Mexican people — ignorant, visionary, sensitive, and enraged against the United States. Whatever their leaders might wish personally — and the sensible ones among them knew what war with the United States would mean — none of them dared defy public opinion in Mexico and receive an American Minister. The bare rumor of such a possibility evoked from Mexican newspapers such comment as this:

The vile government [of Mexico] has been and is in correspondence with the usurpers. The Yankee Parrot [William S. Parrott, a confidential agent of Polk] and the American consul at Mexico are those who have agreed with the government for the loss of Texas, and this same Parrott has departed for the North to say to his government to send a commissioner to make with our government an ignominious treaty on the basis of the surrender of Texas and we know not what other part of the republic. This is as certain as the existence of God in Heaven.

Behind this hysteria was an inkling of the truth. During 1845 Santa Anna was not the man of the hour in Mexico. His personal fortunes, his risings to power and his fallings from power, were as kaleidoscopic as the revolutions of his country. The year 1845 fell in one of his periods of eclipse, when he was living in exile in Havana. A short-lived government headed by General Herrera appears genuinely to have desired peace at any price, and had intimated to Polk that a minister would be received. Polk jumped at the chance, and in the autumn commissioned John Slidell Minister to Mexico.

The written instructions issued to Slidell both summed up a great deal of previous diplomacy and foreshadowed a great deal more. His avowed purpose was the settlement of American claims against the Mexican Government, involving business losses by American citizens during twenty years, due in some cases to arbitrary acts of the Mexican authorities, in others to unofficial violence during the countless Mexican revolutions. Ten years before, Adams had accused Jackson and Van Buren with deliberately keeping the claims unsatisfied so as to work up anti-Mexican feeling in the United States. In point of fact, at that very time an arbitration was being negotiated. It was conducted by two commissioners from each country with an umpire named by the King of Prussia. The commissioners agreed upon payments to Americans amounting to about half a million dollars. The umpire awarded in addition about a million and a half. This was too much for the Mexican treasury to pay, and the undischarged obligation remained a convenient issue which the United States had always ready, should diplomacy demand a crisis. Polk meant to make the most of it. He assumed that Mexico was as good as bankrupt, and his instructions to Slidell disclosed his ulterior purpose. If Mexico, acknowledging Texan independence, would accept the Rio Grande as a boundary, the United States would itself discharge the claims.

But even this "rectification of frontier" was not Polk's dearest aim. While the wrangle over Texas was going on in 1844, this secretive man pondered many things in his own mind and apparently came to an unsuspected conclusion. Turning his eyes towards the West, he saw in imagination the germ of another Texas far away beyond the mountains. Amid the gigantic spaces and the illimitable forests of "the Californias," here and there, was a dwindling Mexican settlement. Once New Spain had made an attempt to occupy that enormous country, but the inspiration died and now its Spanish-Mexican population was a mere handful. Of real government under Mexico, the vast tract had none. Adventurers from the United States had made their way into the storied region, as earlier into Texas. They came in direct defiance of Mexican law and stayed because they dared to, with no rights in the land. The Sacramento Valley gradually became their favorite region. A place called Sutter's Fort — built by a German adventurer who passed himself off as a Frenchman and had been naturalized as a Mexican — was their wonderful Alsatia, "where all the wandering English and American vagabonds found a refuge in which they could not be disturbed by any Mexican authorities." Before Polk became President, things were beginning to stir in the Sacramento Valley. Sir George Simpson, who was in California in 1842, wrote regarding the polyglot adventurer that if Sutter had "the talent and courage to make the most of his position, he is not unlikely to render California a second Texas. Even now the Americans only want a rallying point for carrying into effect their theory that the English race is destined by 'right divine' to expel the Spaniards from their ancient seats — a theory which has already begun to develop itself in more ways than one."

Not really a part of Mexico, the California of 1844 has been well described as a derelict on the sea of international politics, "to be picked up by any adventurer who chose to take it into the port of a strong and stable government." More than once the United States had felt a passing impulse to acquire California. Jackson and Anthony Butler had that purpose in the back of their heads. Webster had talked of it with Lord Ashburton and had learned that England would make no objection. Aberdeen had expressed himself in the same terms. Nevertheless in 1844 there was a persistent rumor in the United States that England was scheming to take possession of California. Later researches have proved that it was quite without foundation. But, like that other British rumor, the great war scare of 1844, it seemed a reality, at least to such men as Polk. On these two foundations — the American movement into the Sacramento Valley and the rumor of a British design to appropriate California — Polk's foreign policy in 1845 was based. Slidell was to inform Mexico that the United States could not allow the Californias to fall into other hands. For

Upper California and New Mexico, he might offer as much as twenty-five million dollars.

Into the shifting scene of Mexican politics stepped John Slidell, the king's pawn in Polk's vision of peaceful imperialism, only to find that Herrera's Government was in a panic. Rumors that it intended to make terms with the United States were creating a furor and a wily military politician, General Paredes, was working in the army for revolution. The Secretary of Foreign Relations almost tearfully besought Slidell to go his way, to remain hidden, to do anything but force the Government's hand! Recognition of him as Minister, at that minute, was not to be dreamed of. To Slidell, a capable but obtuse man, who seems to have been utterly blind to the nature of the situation, the terror of the Government tottering toward its fall was merely "unparalleled bad faith."

While Slidell was thus describing Mexican policy in his dispatches, Paredes raised a revolt, overturned the Government and made himself President. Slidell's prompt demand, under Polk's orders, for recognition or his passports, met the reply that Mexico would make no concessions. His passports were delivered to him in March, 1846.

The failure of Slidell's mission placed Polk in a

quandary. It was plain that the Californias could not be obtained without war. And he was afraid of Congress. Polk knew that, if he were to ask for support in a defensive war to protect Texas from attack, or even on the doubtful question of the Texan boundary, he could rely on a safe majority. The old Texas of Spanish days stopped at the Nueces River. We have seen that the new Texas boldly claimed the whole left bank of the Rio Grande. As a matter of fact, there was a debatable land between the Nueces and the Rio Grande where neither Texas nor Mexico was in control. But numerous American leaders were willing to adopt the Texan claim and stand on the defensive all along the Rio Grande. Calhoun took this position. Nevertheless, eager friend of Texas though he was, he wanted no further campaign of aggrandizement. When it was rumored in Congress that Polk meditated something larger and more sinister than merely the holding the line of the Rio Grande, Calhoun was deeply alarmed and had friendly conferences on this hinted danger with some of his political enemies.

Though Polk had entered on his Mexican negotiations hopeful of a peaceful solution, he did not intend to be caught napping. He had kept a hand behind his back, and in it he held his weapons. For he had put the army and navy in position to strike if necessary and had caused orders to be issued to the Pacific squadron, to the Gulf squadron, and to the army in the Southwest. Preparations were made for a blockade of the east coast of Mexico. General Zachary Taylor, in command in the Southwest, was instructed early in the game to take his forces into Texas. He went thither by sea and in August, 1845, was encamped near Corpus Christi. There he remained until March of the following year.

Since the Mexican Government refused to receive Slidell, Polk decided to proceed to extremities. Even before this Taylor had been ordered to the Rio Grande. It was known that the army had advanced southward when, on May 9, 1846, there was held a Cabinet meeting at which Polk urged upon his ministers a war policy. All the Cabinet agreed with him except George Bancroft, the Secretary of the Navy, who said he would "feel better satisfied in his course if the Mexican forces had, or should, commit any act of hostility."

It would seem that this appeal to the Goddess of Discord was not in vain. The evening of that same day came a dispatch from Taylor announcing a skirmish with the Mexicans on the 24th of April, on the east side of the Rio Grande, in which several Americans had been killed. As if by magic Polk's horizon cleared. Fate had thus suddenly and unexpectedly filled his hand with trumps. He spent Sunday, the 10th of May, on his celebrated war message, and the facts, adroitly stated to suit his plans, were laid before Congress the next day in these words:

The strong desire to establish peace with Mexico on liberal and honorable terms, and the readiness of this Government to regulate and adjust our boundary and other causes of difference with that power on such fair and equitable principles as would lead to permanent relations of the most friendly nature, induced me in September last to seek the reopening of diplomatic relations between the two countries. . . . An envoy of the United States repaired to Mexico with full powers to adjust every existing difference. . . . The Mexican Government not only refused to receive him or listen to his propositions, but after a long continued series of menaces have at last invaded our territory and shed the blood of our fellow-citizens on our own soil. . . .

The movements of the troops [of the United States] to the Del Norte [Rio Grande] was made by the commanding general under positive instructions to abstain from all aggressive acts towards Mexico . . . unless she should declare war or commit acts of hostility indicative of a state of war. . . .

The Mexican forces at Matamoras assumed a belligerent attitude, and on the 12th of April General Ampudia, then in command, notified General Taylor to break up his camp within twenty-four hours and to retire to the Nueces River, and in the event of his failure to comply with these demands announced that arms, and arms alone, must decide the question. But no open act of hostility was committed until the 24th of April. On that day General Arista, who had succeeded to the command of the Mexican forces, communicated to General Taylor that "he considered hostilities commenced and should prosecute them." A party of dragoons of 63 men and officers were on the same day dispatched from the American camp up the Rio del Norte, on its left bank, to ascertain whether the Mexican troops had crossed or were preparing to cross the river, "became engaged with a large body of these troops, and after a short affair, in which some sixteen were killed and wounded, appear to have been surrounded and compelled to surrender." . . .

As war exists, and, notwithstanding all our efforts to avoid it, exists by the act of Mexico herself, we are called upon by every consideration of duty and patriotism to vindicate with decision the honor, the rights, and the interests of our country. . . . I invoke the prompt action of Congress to recognize the existence of war, and to place at the disposition of the Executive the means of prosecuting the war with vigor, and thus hastening the restoration of peace. . . .

This message proved to be a bombshell which blew the opposition to bits. The President was authorized to raise an army of fifty thousand men. Ten million dollars were placed at his disposal. The war fever which started in Congress swept the country. Volunteers flocked to the recruiting stations and with reckless expedition were hurried to the front. The Gulf squadron immediately blockaded the Mexican coast.

Chance had put still another card into Polk's hand. Early in the year an agent of the exiled Santa Anna, Colonel Atocha, had appeared at Washington, seeking an interview with Polk. His aim was to teach Polk how to manage Mexico. What was needed was the high hand. The leaders were willing enough to do all that the United States desired but dared not appear to be yielding. This interview had occurred during the last stage of Slidell's attempt to impose himself as American Minister to Mexico. Let Slidell retire to Vera Cruz, said Atocha, go aboard an American ship of war, and from its deck issue an ultimatum. But even thus the situation could not be saved properly unless that true friend of the United States, the noble Santa Anna, should be restored to power.

Polk listened with intense interest. At the moment he declined to commit himself. But Atocha had made an impression, for shortly afterward Polk suggested to the Cabinet just such a performance by Slidell, warship and all, as the wily Atocha had described. But the Cabinet did not approve, and Polk decided to bide his time.

Now that fate had put the game in his hand, the President, who was not in the least degree blood-thirsty, returned to his old love, and dreamed of gaining his end peacefully after all. A great show of force and coöperation with a bought President at Mexico City — what might not the two accomplish with the minimum loss of blood! On the day on which war was declared the following "private and confidential" order was sent to Commodore Conner of the Gulf squadron: "Commodore: if Santa Anna endeavors to enter the Mexican ports, you will allow him to pass freely."

But such arrangements were not enough. To hasten the peaceful solution, Polk entered into direct negotiation with the rascally Mexican exile at Havana. Commander A. S. Mackenzie, a nephew of Slidell, who was sent to Cuba, discussed with Santa Anna his hypocritical programme of "reforms" and received from him a written statement of what he proposed to do. In this paper Santa Anna declared that "he would not hesitate to make concessions rather than see Mexico" ruined by its present rulers, and that "if the Government of the United States shall promote his patriotic desires, he offers to respond with such a peace as has been described." In this paper Santa Anna advised that Taylor invade Mexico as far as San Luis Potosí, "which movement will compel Mexicans of all parties to recall" Santa Anna. He stipulated that "the greatest secrecy be observed concerning these communications," and he also gave advice about attacking Vera Cruz and the conduct of the blockade.

No European pretender — Stuart, Bourbon, or any other — ever offered to sell out his country with a more barefaced cynicism. No unscrupulous foreign government ever fell into a pretender's trap more easily. Subsequently, as might have been expected, Santa Anna denied ever having had this interview or made these statements. But historians have shown thus far no inclination to accept his word rather than Mackenzie's. Santa Anna's character stands in the way of any such vindication. Furthermore, the preliminary mission of Atocha fits too closely into the circumstantial evidence. Polk himself had no doubt of the accuracy of Mackenzie's report; the orders by which a chink in the blockade was kept open for Santa

Anna's benefit continued in force, and in the middle of August Santa Anna slipped through the chink. Between the lines of Commodore Conner's report, the incident becomes positively comic. Santa Anna was aboard a British ship, the *Arab*, and Conner's silences, if they mean anything, allow us a glimpse of officers of the British and American navies winking at each other with their tongues in their cheeks as the *Arab* gets through the blockade and out again and the Englishmen certify to Conner that the ship carried no freight. By just what sort of "gentlemen's agreement" they manipulated this farce Conner does not say.

Thus Santa Anna came home to Mexico!

CHAPTER XI

"THE HERO OF BUENA VISTA"

THE man who was the striking arm of the United States Government during 1846 was a first-rate soldier, though not much of a general. He was sixty-two years old and had behind him forty years of hard service, chiefly against the Indians. In origin a farmer, he remained to the end the rugged countryman. He despised form, held insignia in contempt, and loved his shirt sleeves. "Old Rough and Ready" was the army's nickname for Zachary Taylor.

The forces which Taylor commanded in the Mexican War at first consisted of a portion of the regular army, rapidly augmented by volunteers. The war fever drew men to the colors from all parts of the country. One of the distinguishing features of this war was the hard fighting endured with honor by American volunteers in their initial engagements. To be sure, these were very different from the scientific movements of the present day. Taylor's battles, especially, depended little upon strategy but for that very reason they tested all the more the mettle of the American temperament — its boldness, its energy, its grimness. Taylor's victories were particularly the victories of the average American soldier.

The petty skirmish which enabled Polk to save his policy occurred while Taylor was entrenching himself near the Rio Grande and was building what is now known as Fort Brown opposite Matamoras. His base of supplies was on the coast at Point Isabel. The importance of the American volunteers in this war was foreshadowed by Taylor's immediate appeal to the Governors of Texas and Louisiana to send him with all possible speed five thousand men.

The Mexicans, whose base was at Matamoras, planned to surround Taylor, cut his connections with Point Isabel, and force his surrender. To frustrate this and to obtain fresh supplies Taylor marched back to Point Isabel on May 1, 1846, leaving a garrison under Major Brown at the fort. The relative movements of the two armies do not reflect credit on their intelligence systems. While Taylor was marching east, he passed, without knowing it, the main body of the Mexican army, which had crossed the river between Fort Brown and Point Isabel. The Mexican General, Arista, hearing of his movements, turned west for an attack on the fort, whose present name commemorates ¡the death of Major Brown in the gallant repulse of the Mexicans.

On the 7th of May, with two hundred wagons and over two thousand men, Taylor, like the noble Duke of York in the familiar rhyme, prepared to march back again. But Arista got wind of his intention and prepared for a battle at a place called Palo Alto. There Taylor encountered him on the 8th of May. The little battle which followed, though it has been made a great action by fervid describers, ended with the fall of night and left neither side victorious. But after sharp experience of the Americans at short range, the Mexicans, though technically undefeated, thought they had had enough of it, and at dawn began an orderly retreat. The American soldier rather than his general, morale rather than strategy, had triumphed. By ten o'clock on the 9th of May the Mexicans had withdrawn to a new position five miles nearer the river and were in camp along a ravine not far from the Resaca de la Palma.

Taylor followed deliberately, and not until late afternoon was fighting resumed. This time the Americans really won the battle. Arista, who did not expect an attack that day, had made no preparations. As the sun began to sink, he was in his tent writing. His men, greatly depressed by their experience at Palo Alto, were cooking their suppers. The horses were unsaddled. Into this dismal but unsuspecting army there dropped the sudden fire of the advancing American infantry, followed by sharp fighting sustained by the Mexican outposts and then a staggering cavalry charge led by Captain May of the American regulars. A panic, a stampede — and the Mexicans had abandoned the field. Arista retreated into Mexico, since, with his demoralized army, he found it impossible to hold Matamoras, and Taylor took possession of the place.

While Taylor was feeling his way southward through eastern Mexico, two raids farther west revealed the fact that all northwestern Mexico was without troops for its defense. From Fort Leavenworth, early in the summer, Colonel Stephen W. Kearny led forth an expedition that would have been one of the follies of history had it not been inspired by accurate knowledge of Mexico and the

Mexicans. Aiming at nothing less than the conquest of New Mexico and with no base of supplies behind him, Kearny took barely sufficient food to carry him to Santa Fé. His faith in his own judgment was justified by the surrender of Santa Fé the moment he appeared before it. Having proclaimed all New Mexico a part of the United States, Kearny turned westward across the horizon of the present narrative and rode blithely into the little side war then raging in California.[1] In the autumn and early winter General Wool, starting from San Antonio, marched three hundred miles to the Mexican town of Parras, whence he made a wide sweep eastward and eventually joined Taylor's army without encountering serious opposition at any point.

Now to return to the main army. For nearly four months Taylor was making ready for a further advance into Mexico. Though his enemies did not molest him, he had great difficulties. In everything but fighting the American army was inefficient. Sickness, inadequate transport, and congestion at every possible point made a dreary record for the summer of 1846. Meanwhile

[1] See *The Forty-Niners*, by Stewart Edward White (in *The Chronicles of America*).

volunteers poured into Taylor's camp faster than he could provide for them. Too often the new-comer went directly to the hospital — or what passed muster for a hospital. "The mortality in our camp," wrote an eye-witness, "was appalling. The dead march was ever wailing in our ears and even at this distant period, I can scarcely look back to our stay there without a shudder. . . . Large hospital tents were constantly full — the dead being removed at sunrise and sunset but to make room for the dying. The groans and lamentations of the poor sufferers during those sickly sultry nights were heart-rending."

Taylor had fixed on the city of Monterey as his next objective. Early in September, with about six thousand effective troops, he was on the march. On the nineteenth, he approached the city and went into camp about three miles to the northeast. Monterey lay on a plain, open on the north but inclosed by mountains on the other three sides. The enemy had made the most of these natural defenses and were present in force. Taylor divided his army into two sections — one under his immediate command and the other under General William J. Worth, who was ordered to make a detour around the north side of the city and to attack from the west, cutting the road from Monterey to Saltillo. These two commanders attacked the town from opposite sides and each fought his own battle with but little knowledge of the movements of the other. The conduct of the men was above praise. Danger seemed a meaningless word to them. Death they had forgotten. During the 21st, 22d, and 23d of September the Americans fought their way into the city, from both sides, in the most gallant fashion, foot by foot. On the morning of the twenty-fourth General Ampudia, with his surviving troops cooped up in the center of the town, asked for terms. Taylor did not insist on an unconditional surrender but accepted an agreement to evacuate with a temporary cessation of hostilities. Thus Ampudia withdrew, leaving the Americans in possession of Monterey.

The sheer hard fighting at Monterey and the capture of the city naturally impressed the American people, and they accepted the commanding general as a conquering hero. The Administration, however, saw the situation in other colors. "In agreeing to this armistice," Polk wrote in his diary, "General Taylor violated his express orders and I regret that I cannot approve of his course. He had the enemy in his power and should have taken them prisoners. . . . It will only enable the Mexican army to reorganize and recruit so as to make another stand." Polk's irritation and anxiety were due in part to the turn that had been given to affairs by the course of Santa Anna. That slippery intriguer had done what might have been expected of him — had broken all his promises to Polk, had put himself at the head of the military party in Mexico, and was now making ready for what looked like determined war. Polk realized what a vain folly had been his game with Santa Anna. He saw, too, that more troops must be sent to Mexico. There must be more hard fighting. Would Congress stand by him? How exasperating at such a moment to hear that Taylor for the second time had failed to strike a body blow.

Thenceforth, the Administration had no good word for Taylor. It must be admitted that Taylor's dispatches during the remainder of the year contained nothing to commend him. They were often querulous, sometimes ill-tempered, always weighted with advice about the further conduct of the war. These plans were often patently unwise and revealed Taylor's poor understanding of strategy. He was a splendid fighter — just the man to take a city by storm — but an inferior general.

ZACHARY TAYLOR

Painting by G. P. A. Healy, after Amans. In the Corcoran Gallery of Art, Washington.

Polk had now lost faith in Taylor. Gradually, under other advice, the President developed a new plan of campaign. In November it was decided to invade Mexico from the sea. Vera Cruz was to be taken as the base of operations. The command of this ambitious expedition was entrusted to General Winfield Scott. Late in the month, dispatches were sent to Taylor informing him of the plan, in which he was to play the inferior rôle of maintaining a threatening attitude on the northern flank of Mexico. The real business was now the Vera Cruz expedition. Taylor was, therefore, to send every man he could spare to the coast, whence they would be forwarded to Scott.

During this period of uncertainty at Washington, Taylor had pursued a course which Polk interpreted as paying " no regard to the views of the Government." While not exactly disobeying the War Department, Taylor had treated its advice as of little consequence. He had pushed forward his advance guard to the Mexican town of Saltillo and was holding what Washington considered an exposed position in defiance of the wishes of the War Department. There were now under Taylor's command several distinct units which he had placed at widely distant points on a line nearly five hundred miles long running from the sea at Tampico through Monterey and Saltillo far into the interior of Mexico. "General Taylor by dispersing his forces into small bodies," wrote Polk in his diary, "has acted directly against the views of the Government and contrary to his own views as communicated to the Government that he could not advance beyond Monterey with safety."

During December Taylor himself became convinced that he had not disposed his forces well. He was busily rearranging his disposition, when, after singular delays, he received in January, 1847, imperative orders subordinating him to Scott. Taylor thereupon sent a bitter dispatch to Scott saying he could not "misunderstand the object of the arrangement" showing that he had "lost the confidence of the Government" — which was quite true.

Though Taylor obeyed the unconditional part of his new instructions, he continued to disregard advice. Scott urged him to fall back from Saltillo and to concentrate at Monterey. It is possible that Taylor, bitterly mortified by the action of the Government, was rendered stubborn by this advice. At any rate, he took the opposite course. Drawing together what he could of the troops left to him, he passed beyond Saltillo and went as far as a place called Agua Nueva, where he maintained his headquarters from the 5th to the 21st of February. The force under his immediate command was smaller than when he began the march to Monterey. It consisted of little over forty-seven hundred men, some of whom were quite raw.

While Taylor was thus exposing himself to the danger of an attack by a rapid concentration of the enemy, Santa Anna was leading northward by way of San Luis Potosí a force which outnumbered Taylor's three to one. On the 20th of February, Taylor heard that Santa Anna had passed San Luis Potosí and was moving straight toward him, while two thousand cavalry under General Miñon were circling through the mountains to the east of Saltillo, which was still his main depot of supplies. On the following day, Taylor's scouts sighted Miñon to the eastward, while to the south they made out the advance of Santa Anna. As Agua Nueva was no place for a defensive battle, Taylor was at last compelled to take the advice he had hitherto scorned and retire to safer ground.

From Agua Nueva a highroad ran north eighteen miles to Saltillo through a broad pass in the mountains. The character of this pass determined the course of the battle which forms the concluding incident in Taylor's military career. Taylor marched back twelve miles to the hacienda of Buena Vista near the northern end of the pass. He was unable to remove all the supplies collected at Agua Nueva but carried off a portion in wagon trains at "furious speed" and ordered the rear guard to destroy the remainder. At daybreak on the 22d of February, the whole American army was gathered about Buena Vista.

Looking back over the course of his retreat, the course which Santa Anna might be expected to follow, Taylor pondered certain features of its topography but failed entirely to allow for certain others. He disposed his forces in an unfortunate way. The scene before him, as he saw it, had three main characteristics. First, the average level of the pass was a flat though deeply crevassed plain, lying north and south and bounded on either hand by mountains of considerable height. The space between the mountains varied in width from a mile and a half to five miles. In the second place, the crevasses worn in this plain by watercourses were not only deep but were also of a peculiar formation, the most important one, as Taylor thought, having its bottom sixty to seventy feet below the average

level of the plain. The earthen cliffs that formed
the walls of these crevasses were as a rule very
nearly perpendicular. The geological explanation
is that frost, with its corroding and crumbling
effects on earthen banks, is in that region almost
unknown. The mountain torrents cut their way
through the plains as neatly as if the cutting had
been done by a gardener's spade, and their banks
remain perpendicular, like the banks of a well-kept
ditch. For an advancing force of infantry to de-
scend one side of these crevasses and ascend the
other without the aid of scaling-ladders would be
extremely difficult, especially along the deep parts
of the crevasses. For cavalry or artillery, it would
in many places be impossible.

The third thing which Taylor perceived correctly
was the relation of the highroad from Agua Nueva
to this system of crevasses and their watercourses.
There was a main stream through the pass and a
number of tributaries. The main stream followed
closely the western ridge, running along its foot
and leaving almost the whole of the plain of the
pass between it and the eastern ridge. Through
the crevasse or miniature canyon of this main
stream the road came northward toward Taylor's
eye, in a narrow passage between the water and

the perpendicular earthen cliffs. To a man standing in the road by the stream side, the tops of the
earthen cliffs which formed the banks of the crevasse ditch appeared to be more than forty feet
above his head, level with the plain of the pass, and
by looking over his left shoulder, he could see a
long distance through lateral crevasses of apparently equal depth reaching off toward the eastern
mountains — other miniature canyons whose floors
joined that of the main canyon through which ran
the stream and the highway. Such were the three
characteristics of the scene which Taylor grasped.
But there was still a fourth, more vital than the
others, which he failed to grasp.

The field of battle, as Taylor conceived it, was
to be a new Thermopylæ. Owing to lateral crevasses, which appeared to the American general to
be impassable, Santa Anna with his cavalry and
his artillery would have no choice but to advance
along the highroad, through the sunken corridor.
Thus the coming fight would involve a grim defense of a narrow passage — as at Thermopylæ,
with its narrow passage between mountain and sea
— and Santa Anna might come to his destruction
between the river and the cliff and be welcome.
There, as Taylor saw it, was the key to the coming

battle and there he posted the artillery upon which he chiefly relied — eight guns under Captain Washington. The bulk of the American army was drawn up on the left of Washington and in his rear. The troops to the left were mainly on the plain, high above Washington's head, along the brink of a crevasse. In their rear were two light batteries commanded by Captain William T. Sherman and Captain Braxton Bragg. Neither to the right nor to the left did the American line extend the whole way to the mountains that formed the parallel walls of the pass, though far to the left near the base of the mountains was an outpost of cavalry and four companies of foot.

Let us now reverse the point of view and look upon the scene with the eyes of Santa Anna as he came up through the pass from the south. Though not a great general, Santa Anna was no fool. To march on along the sunken road to a Homeric slaughter in front of Washington's guns, as Taylor was inviting him to do, was quite too obviously a case of the spider and the fly. Santa Anna and his officers also observed the topography of the pass and promptly seized upon the fourth characteristic, which Taylor had overlooked. The lateral crevasses, far back at the heads of their watercourses, became shallow. Along the foot of the eastern mountains, before the water, in its rush toward the main stream, had cut deep into the plain, there was a strip of land where the crevasses were not sufficiently deep to impede the movements of troops. There and not at the Thermopylæ of the highroad, lay the real key to the situation. The topography of the land made it necessary for any one attempting to hold this pass against attack to fight simultaneously two battles — one down in the corridor of the stream to hold control of the road, and another at some distance to the east to hold the open country at the heads of the lateral crevasses. Between the two positions lay the impassable region of the deep crevasses with their nearly perpendicular walls.

The battle of Buena Vista consisted of four stages. The first comprised the American preparations; the second, the first Mexican attack which promptly revealed the faultiness of Taylor's plan; the third, Taylor's rearrangement of his forces. These three stages occurred on the 22d of February. The fourth, the knock-down fight under conditions Taylor had not foreseen, occurred the next day.

The second stage of the battle consisted of a

WINFIELD SCOTT

Engraving after a daguerreotype taken at the time of the Mexican War. In the Print Department of the New York Public Library.

WINFIELD SCOTT

Engraving after a daguerreotype taken at the time of the
Mexican War. In the Print Department of the New York Public
Library.

Gravure, Andersen-Lamb Co. N.Y.

quiet movement of the Mexican troops by means of the shallow ends of the lateral crevasses on to the lower slopes of the eastern mountains and toward the open country. The Mexicans meant to turn the American position from the east, and, while the Americans guarding the road were held in their Thermopylæ by a frontal attack, to envelop the entire army caught in its own net.

The instant the Americans perceived this purpose the third stage of the battle began. Taylor had been involved in his own imperfect strategy. His efforts to rectify his mistake late in the day demanded radical changes in the arrangement of the American troops. It was obvious now that the main battle would be the eastern one and would be fought at the heads of the crevasses. Taylor accordingly withdrew three of Washington's guns from the road, hurried them up to the plain, and sent them eastward to the region where the advancing Mexicans, now established on the mountains, threatened to accomplish their flanking design. To support the guns he sent other reënforcements in the same direction. At the same time, as if fearful that he had been caught napping at each end of his line, Taylor ordered part of Bragg's artillery with a supporting force to cross the stream and

14

take position in the other gap he had left open at the far edge of the strip of fields along the foot of the ridge on the west.

These movements and counter-movements, involving some desultory firing at long range with little serious result, filled the 22d of February. At nightfall Taylor had rearranged his army and had partially closed the gap between the heads of the crevasses and the eastern mountains. But this crucial ground was not really in his possession. The Mexicans were on the slopes of the mountains still farther to the east in an admirable position to carry out their plan of turning the flank of the Americans.

During the night the American commander went back to Saltillo to make sure that all was well at his base. He was not on the field when the real battle began at dawn on the 23d of February. On that day the two actions which nature had foreordained took place. The one on the road was not seriously pressed by the Mexicans. Knowing the American position to be impregnable, they contented themselves with enough of a demonstration to keep the defenders at their posts. The real battle was an ebb and flow — backwards by the Americans from the heads of the crevasses to the hacienda and forward again to their original position. This eastward battle was opened by skirmishing on the mountains, followed by a great rush of Mexicans along the lower slopes and through the open strip at their feet. The most exposed American troops at that moment were the gunners of the three cannon sent thither the night before and some Indiana volunteers supporting them. In a furious combat these checked the Mexicans for a few moments but were soon driven back with the loss of one of the guns. Every man and horse belonging to it had been killed or disabled. As these exposed Americans fell back while the bulk of the Mexican army continued its circling movement along the base of the mountains, there could no longer be any doubt where the battle was going to be lost or won. The thin American line which the night before had been thrown so hastily across from the crevasse heads to the mountains, as an obstacle to the Mexican advance, must be saved at all cost. Sherman accordingly pushed all his guns forward. Bragg and his Kentucky volunteers, who had been sent across to the western mountain slopes at nightfall, were now hastily recalled and hurried off to the extreme east.

But before the reinforcements could make their

presence felt, the mischief had been done. The Mexicans had burst through the American line. The American skirmishers on the extreme east were cut off from the main army. Looking back, they saw the struggling American line swinging like a gate on a pivot where, at the right hand, it touched the deep section of a crevasse, swinging back, back, from its original position at right angles to the mountains until the gate was open and the way was free for the Mexicans. To reach their comrades the skirmishers had to run for it, making a wide detour, getting ahead of the advancing Mexicans, and then racing right across their path. Their escape was made possible only by the brief, desperate interruption of the Mexican advance when Bragg and Sherman got into action.

The whole eastward battle by this time had the look of an American defeat. The Mexicans, pouring now along the base of the mountains through the wide open gateway around the heads of the crevasses, appeared to have the success of their encircling movement within easy reach. On the left, the backward swinging American line was approaching the hacienda. The loss of the Americans in killed and wounded had been heavy. Their formations were more or less disorganized. Indeed, some Americans were running, and these "strag-glers," racing past the hacienda, did not pause until they reached Saltillo, where they reported the destruction of the American army.

It was in this desperate moment when the battle appeared to be lost that Taylor returned to the field after his night at the base of supplies. The grim old Indian fighter found now just the situa-tion in which he appeared at his best. Arriving at the hacienda, he saw the vicinity occupied by sol-diers slowly retreating in confusion. But close at hand fortunately was the regiment of Mississippi Rifles commanded by Jefferson Davis. With these and with the reserves which had hitherto supported Washington's battle but which were now brought up to save the other engagement, the Mexican ad-vance was checked. A quick reorganization of the confused troops surrounding the hacienda and a swift counterstroke converted the check into a retirement. The Mexicans drew back.

While the Mexicans paused, Taylor completed the reorganization of the eastward battle and pre-pared for an heroic attempt to regain his position — to turn his line back on its pivot at the deep crevasse, to swing the gate shut against the enemy. This was the time for a supreme stroke on the part of the Mexicans; but they missed their chance. Hovering along the base of the mountains, they foolishly satisfied themselves with cavalry charges. One detachment of cavalry swept right through the hacienda, reached the stream, crossed it, rode completely around the American army, and then made its way along the western mountains to a juncture with the Mexicans before Washington.

Another downpour of Mexican horsemen created the military reputation of Jefferson Davis. Across their path was drawn Davis' command and the third Indiana regiment. Coming down on the gallop, the Mexicans did not like the look of that line of silent Americans, motionless in the open. The Mexican leaders shortened rein and rode warily. Then they halted. At that moment the word of command ran along the American line. There was the spitting crackle of the deadly American fire. Mexican saddles were emptied. Horses plunged and ran masterless. The surviving Mexicans jerked their horses round and rode hard for the mountains.

Now, too late, Santa Anna threw all his reserves into the eastward battle which became a furious fight in the contracted area between the crevasse heads and the mountains. The superior mettle of the Americans determined the outcome. Though the Mexicans had numbers on their side, they were slowly and steadily pushed back. By nightfall they had been driven around the heads of the crevasses and off the lower slopes of the mountains. The return movement of the Americans, still pivoted at the right hand on the flanking crevasse, had succeeded. The gate had been swung back and was now shut against the Mexicans. As darkness fell, the two armies stood practically where they had stood the night before. The net result of the twenty-four hours since the battle began was apparently nothing at all — except for the miseries of the wounded and the tragic peace of the dead.

If the Mexicans, with their great advantage in numbers, should prove equal to the occasion, what were Taylor's chances for the morrow? But the Mexicans had no stomach for more fighting. By this time their morale was exhausted. In the night under a pale moon Santa Anna with all his army stole off on a forced march back to San Luis Potosí. When morning dawned, the Americans were without adversaries. Taylor instantly sent off dispatches proclaiming a splendid victory. The American public went wild and in due time gave the commander his reward by making him President of the United States.

CHAPTER XII

THE STROKE FROM THE EAST

GENERAL WINFIELD SCOTT, whom Polk had reluctantly placed in command of his invading army — for Polk was a strict party man of the old sort and Scott was a Whig — was a brilliant, elderly dandy. He loved fine uniforms. Afoot, his figure was criticized as being short in the leg; but this defect enhanced his appearance mounted, especially when he rode a big horse and "towered," as the comment was, resplendent. He had the dandy's traditional courage. As a young man in the war of 1812 he had made a name for himself as a gallant soldier. At sixty he was an accomplished student of the art of war, and was well versed in the theories accepted by his time. He knew something of European travel. There was a dash of the writer in him. His intellect, though deliberate, was powerful. He had a shrewd eye for men. To sum up the characteristics that made for his advantage, he was talented, cultivated, impressive, debonair.

Unfortunately there was another side to Scott. He was vain, and a love of flattery was one of his dangers. There were circumstances in which his temper could not be relied upon. The incipient writer, caged so to speak in the soldier, sometimes broke free, rash and undisciplined, with results that in one case at least were appalling — as will be seen in the marvellous letter that must be quoted toward the end of this chapter. Altogether, good qualities and bad, Winfield Scott inspired one of his ablest critics to compare him with General Webb in Thackeray's *Henry Esmond*. The comparison is a happy one. George Lockhart Rives penetrates Scott's character when he says, "those lines which pleased Webb so highly might well have been written of Scott:

"Before the front the general sternly rides
  With such an air as Mars to battle strides;
  Propitious heaven must sure a hero save,
  Like Paris handsome and like Hector brave."

The brilliant qualities of Scott were in evidence during the early part of his invasion. From his rendezvous at Lobos Island, off the Mexican coast to the south of Tampico, he sailed with a great fleet of transports to Vera Cruz. One of the thrilling moments for the American army was that in which Scott's landing parties entered their boats, a few miles south of Vera Cruz, facing an open beach backed by a line of sand hills behind which for all they knew might be the whole Mexican army.[1] Amid loud cheers from the ships, over a glistening sea, the boats raced for the beach. The first boat to touch carried the commanding officer, General Worth — fighting Worth of Monterey — who was the first man ashore. Leaping overboard in shallow water, forming instantly in a battle line, the Americans charged the sandhills, topped them, and faced — an empty landscape. An anticlimax, to be sure, but with no element of the unheroic.

Scott promptly invested Vera Cruz. After four days' bombardment, during which the city was ruined while the American loss was trifling, Vera Cruz surrendered. No Mexican forces had approached to relieve the city; there was no evidence that any notable army threatened him; and yet at hand on the coast was an enemy that Scott rightly feared. This was yellow fever. His next aim,

[1] A party of Mexican cavalry had been driven from the beach by cannon fire.

therefore, was to clear Vera Cruz and get up into the mountains before the fever appeared on the coast, and in this he succeeded and so saved his army.

The American invaders set out for "the City," the capital of Mexico, following much the line which Cortés had taken three hundred years before. A charming record of this great march has been preserved in the letters of a young artillery captain to his wife. Robert Anderson, afterward Major Anderson of Fort Sumter fame, looked upon the road through Mexico with the eye of the imagination. Witness his suggested contrast of past and present, in connection with what was known as the National Bridge whence he "went to visit an old fortification intended to command the approaches to the bridge. The fort is an old one on a high hill, the side pretty well defended by musquetry fires. This place we learned had been furnished with eight pieces of artillery which were withdrawn the day before. . . . The scenery at the bridge is beautiful. . . . The bridge is like all of the Spanish works of art constructed during their stay in this country, well executed and on a magnificent scale."

Even the bravest of the Americans, in whom fear

had no place, might well congratulate themselves as they wound up and up into rugged and still more rugged mountains, where impregnable positions were without defenders, that they faced the present of Santa Anna and not the past of Cortés.

Meanwhile what was Santa Anna about? This enigmatic man has received no serious consideration from American historians. The tradition has been that he does not deserve any, and he is pictured as a common fraud, alternately boasting and running away. His own defense is based on the cowardice of his armies, which, he insists, compelled him often to flee or be taken, and he chose not to be taken. Nevertheless, no matter who was responsible for the Mexican panic after that drawn battle of Buena Vista, Santa Anna had rallied a considerable force at San Luis Potosí. Military problems and a crisis in Mexican politics had delayed his subsequent movements and for these reasons Scott had not been molested at Vera Cruz. But now Santa Anna had organized another army, had weathered his political crisis, and was about to challenge Scott's advance.

Against the advice of his chief engineer, Santa Anna fortified the pass of Cerro Gordo on the main road to Puebla. The choice of ground was unwise for several reasons, especially, as the event proved, because in case of disaster it would be impossible to retreat, so narrow was the only exit backward from the Mexican position. The Mexican leader nevertheless placed his army in a segment of high broken country, the hollow of an arc of mountains whose chord was a line of precipices six hundred feet deep forming the canyon of a river. Between the precipices and the mountains Scott was advancing along a zigzag road. The right wing of the Mexican line rested on the precipices, whence it stretched diagonally across the segment to the mountains in such a way that most of the Mexicans had the precipices at their backs. Santa Anna did not consider it worth while to occupy the lower slopes of the mountains so as to make impossible any attempt on the part of the Americans to turn his left wing, because he thought not even a rabbit could get over such difficult ground.

Among the Americans, however, a young engineer disagreed with Santa Anna. The opinion of Captain Robert E. Lee, that the Americans could make their way along the mountain slopes and turn the Mexican left, was accepted by Scott, who gave orders for the hazardous undertaking. The plan involved two attacks: at a set time the

Americans were to assail the front of the Mexicans, while at the same time the flanking column was to attack from the rear.

The all but insuperable difficulty of this flanking movement along the mountain slope made a deep impression upon another young American officer, Lieutenant Ulysses S. Grant, who subsequently described this march "over chasms where the walls were so steep men could barely climb them. Animals could not. . . . The engineers, who had directed the opening, led the way and the troops followed. Artillery was let down the steep sides by hand, the men engaged attaching a strong rope to the rear axle and letting the guns down, a piece at a time, while men at the ropes kept their ground at the top, paying out gradually, while a few at the front directed the course of the piece. In like manner the guns were drawn by hand up the opposite slopes."

A day and a night were necessary for the accomplishment of this operation. A Mexican detachment which discovered the Americans was put to flight, and an outlying Mexican fortification was taken by storm. Early the next morning, Sunday, the 18th of April, the separate parts of Scott's army began their attacks according to schedule.

The flanking column hurled itself on the left wing of the Mexicans, crushed it, and sent the survivors whirling through the narrow exit along the precipices which was their one escape. Having penetrated the Mexican line to the brink of the precipices, the American flanking column now held the bulk of their enemies in a trap. Meanwhile the Mexicans of the center and the right had also been attacked by Scott's other columns so that now in front and on each side of them were the American bayonets and at their back was the line of precipices. Their comrades of the left wing had already saved themselves by running, and these men, thus trapped, threw down their arms. Santa Anna, however, was not with them. The flight of his left wing had carried him along with it, and he was now riding hard for safety. Scott had nothing further to do with him for several months. The only effective Mexican force between the American army and Mexico City was thus destroyed, and its artillery, ammunition, and supplies were all in the hands of the conqueror.

The Americans now pushed on to Jalapa — "the beautiful and celebrated city of Jalapa," Anderson calls it. The next evening, he writes, his command encamped "near a large cotton factory; the night was intensely cold, ice formed in our basins." Two days afterward, writing from the historic Castle of Perote, he describes the march from the camp near the cotton factory.

Off again, the next morning early, road ascending and rough; about eleven we came to a village at the entrance to a pass which they had commenced fortifying, but seized by the panic spread by the runaways from the battle of Cerro Gordo, they had abandoned it, leaving seven or eight pieces of cannon on the ground. This would have been an ugly pass, as it is in the midst of the lava of an old volcano, exceedingly rough and sharp; its rough jagged points would have impeded the advance of our troops and kept us under their fire.

Passing over this volcanic road, we soon found ourselves in the region of the pine. The scenery was exceedingly grand and picturesque. Encamped that night at Las Vegas, water excellent, night cold. The next day we entered this celebrated work early in the day, the troops having hastily abandoned it the preceding day. We are now in the region of the cedar.

Scott's immediate objective was Puebla, where he intended drawing a long breath before proceeding to the extremity. Anderson gives interesting details of the march. On the 7th of May, he writes:

A command of two companies of infantry and one of dragoons was sent forward this morning on the Puebla

road, some fifteen miles, to bring an Alcade, or some of his subjects, to task for preventing the inhabitants around the town from bringing provisions to the troops here. . . . Our paying the Mexicans liberally for what they bring will induce them to come, our punishing those who prevent them will show them that . . . our strength . . . will be exerted when necessity demands it. . . . The market people are becoming much more reasonable in their prices; we now buy a dozen eggs for eighteen and three quarters cents, occasionally five cents for a pie; onions, sixteen for six and one quarter cents, and bananas, seven for six and one quarter cents. Chickens half grown, eighteen and three quarters cents *each*. These prices will do very well. The fresh meats we get are generally hog and sheep — the hogs always skinned — most funny looking things they are with their jackets off. In this region we scarcely ever see a cow.

When we remember what havoc invading armies have made in our own time, we find Anderson's intimate account of the tranquillity of Puebla under the American rule refreshing.

Scott held Puebla about three months, from the middle of May until near the middle of August. During this period the less fortunate side of his character became manifest. He was deeply worried over problems of supply and allowed them to get on his nerves. One-year volunteers whose terms of enlistment were about to expire had to be released and sent back to the coast. The War Department was slow in replacing these men—not, apparently, through the fault of any one in particular but merely through the general unpreparedness that has always characterized the entry of the United States into a war. These delays and disappointments upset Scott's temper. He wrote savagely to the War Department accusing it of a plot to "destroy" him by withholding reinforcements. It was during this period of tense strain that a certain Nicholas P. Trist made his appearance at Puebla. And thereby hangs a tale — a tale that takes us back to Washington.

Months before, while Scott was assembling his forces for the invasion, who should reappear at Washington but Colonel Atocha. He had the same old story to tell. Santa Anna in his heart longed for peace, peace at the American price — but under present conditions he dared not propose it to the Mexican people. Stale as the bait was, Polk rose to it a second time. He discussed with his Cabinet the question of sending a plenipotentiary to the front armed with extraordinary powers both diplomatic and military.

Polk and his Cabinet, one of the least distinguished in the annals of American politics, now embarked on a surprising course of mistaken diplomacy. First they tried some backstairs negotiations in which they used Atocha — that shady diplomat, once the personal representative of the leader of the nation with which they were at war! — as the go-between. Atocha made his way to Mexico City, where he gave out that the United States Government demanded the cession of all Mexico north of a line drawn due west from the mouth of the Rio Grande, along the twenty-sixth parallel, in return for fifteen million dollars. In March the envoy was back at Washington with the refusal of the Mexican Government to consider such terms, and the note from Mexico was bitter, not to say insolent.

Meanwhile rumors had got abroad that the President was in favor of immense conquests in Mexico. Calhoun took alarm. From the first he had opposed a war of conquest. To safeguard Texas and secure a strategical frontier — that was all he would approve. Distrusting the President, he introduced resolutions in the Senate, in 1847, condemning the idea of extensive Mexican conquests. Nearly a year before, when Polk seems to have favored the line through the mouth of the Rio Grande, Calhoun had come out in support of a line following the Rio Grande from its mouth to El Paso del Norte and thence due west to the sea.

Polk, always solicitous lest a defection among his Democratic followers in Congress should leave him helpless, decided to limit his demands to a cession which should be bounded as Calhoun indicated: Mexico should cede the east bank of the Rio Grande, New Mexico, Upper California, and also Lower California. To bring this about, a plenipotentiary was to go to the front, with power not only to treat for peace but, if necessary, to order the commanding general to cease hostilities. For this extraordinary mission Polk selected no high official but a mere clerk in the State Department. Nicholas P. Trist was a capable clerk, to be sure, and a good Democrat, related by marriage to Jefferson, but in the world's eye he was nobody. Could anything but a total lack of imagination explain the dispatch of such an envoy empowered to manipulate a sensitive and harassed general, proud of a great achievement?

Trist proceeded to Vera Cruz and sent a letter to Scott announcing his approach and the nature of his mission. Scott received this letter at Jalapa and wrote an irritated, unbecoming reply. While Scott was still there, Trist overtook the army but did not present himself to the commanding general, and for several days the envoy and the general remained in the same town without meeting. Then Scott left for Puebla. Two letters from Trist, who lingered at Jalapa, called forth that letter from Scott which ranks high among historical indiscretions:

My first impulse was to return the farrago of insolence, conceit, and arrogance to the author; but, on reflection, I have determined to preserve the letters as a choice specimen of diplomatic literature and manners. The jacobin convention of France never sent to one of its armies in the field a more amiable and accomplished instrument. If you were but armed with an ambulatory guillotine you would be the personification of Danton, Marat, and St. Just all in one.

You tell me that you are authorized to negotiate a treaty of peace with the enemy, a declaration which, as it rests upon your own word, I might well question; and you add that it was not intended at Washington that I should have anything to do with the negotiation. This I can well believe, and certainly have cause to be thankful to the President for not degrading me by placing me in any joint commission with you.

In the middle of May, Trist reached Puebla. Until almost the end of June he and Scott were not on speaking terms. During this time a ridiculous three-cornered discussion between Scott, Trist, and the Administration formed an episode which Americans today would like to forget. From it no one issued with credit. Scott's resentment went so far that he wrote to Washington asking to be relieved. The President, unable to see that his own wooden-headedness was the cause of the trouble, berated Scott in his diary and longed for some one he dared put in his place.

This disgraceful situation changed color suddenly, like a stage transformation scene, just as June closed. For some reason not yet known Scott and Trist faced about and became friends. Presently Trist was writing to Washington that his first impression of Scott was all wrong and that the General's "conduct has been characterized by the purest public spirit, and a fidelity and devotion that could not be surpassed to the views of the Government." Scott for his part wrote of the happy change in his relations with Trist, whom he now considered "able, discreet, courteous, and amiable." Both asked to have their previous letters removed from the archives. Was ever diplomacy in such fashion made a laughing stock?

An incident of the reconciliation, and possibly one of its causes, was a visit to Puebla of an attaché of the British legation. Trist, while he and

Scott were at outs, had applied to the British Minister to put him into communication with the Mexican authorities. Adroit management by the Englishman of this difficult situation, together with the opportune reconciliation of the American chiefs, made possible a real, though underhand, negotiation with Santa Anna. Open negotiations would begin if Scott and Trist would promise Santa Anna a million dollars, in perfect secrecy, to be paid when the treaty should be ratified, and if they would provide him at once with ten thousand dollars, all for the purpose of quelling opposition. Scott and Trist fell into the trap. The ten thousand dollars were sent forward. But the open negotiations promised were not begun. Santa Anna resorted to his old subterfuge, which somehow seems always to have deceived the Americans. A more imperative display of force must be made. Scott must threaten the capital more obviously. When the Americans were at the gates, Santa Anna would at last be in a position to defy his domestic enemies and to meet the American demands.

Just how far Scott was taken in has never been determined. His subsequent course of action is often bewildering, and no theory satisfactorily explains all of it. Did he believe that he had fought his last battle and that Santa Anna was virtually his accomplice, or did he see through the wily Mexican? Did Scott think another blow was necessary and that then Santa Anna would keep his word and peace on good terms would follow? Or did the various possibilities leave him so in doubt that he began his advance without any definite forecast of the future?

The one absolutely certain thing is that on August 7, 1847, the American army, consisting now of 10,738 men in splendid condition, abandoned its connection with the coast and marched out of Puebla on its way to the City of Mexico.

CHAPTER XIII

THE PIVOTAL ACTION

Between Puebla and the City of Mexico towers a
wall of mountains capped with perpetual ice. Toward this gigantic fortification the Americans advanced, prepared at every step for battle. From
height to height they rose, wondering whether they
would have to fight again as they had done at
Cerro Gordo. But they encountered no resistance
and on the 10th of August the advance guard
reached the pass for which they had aimed, 10,500
feet above sea-level, with the colossal ice-peak,
Iztaccihuatl, on their left hand. Anderson, describing the arrival of his command at the pass,
writes:

At ten o'clock precisely, . . . my eyes caught the first
view of the valley of Mexico. There it lay, as seen
through the narrow opening made by the road, in the
overhanging trees; a quiet landscape having in the
foreground a sheet of waters; the portion of the valley

visible blending itself imperceptibly in distant mountains, which could scarcely be distinguished, the day being at that moment cloudy, with a gentle mist from the mountains which rested on their sides.

Every turn of the road now opened to us a new or more extensive view . . . every variety of green that could be formed by the varied light and shade of passing clouds . . . mountains here, nearly in the foreground, there, in the distance, and beyond limiting the view; and lake, in this part almost undistinguishable from the grass and slime, which nearly covered it, to the clear water, in which the shadows of the passing clouds were visible; the picture studded with *haciendas*, some traced out by their huge mud walls enclosing immense courtyards, like fortifications, villages with churches, etc., presented views which were charming to those who hoped that there lay the City, from which they *must* return to their beloved homes.

To the military mind the most important geographical feature before the invaders was Lake Texcoco, which lay immediately east of the City of Mexico — that is, between it and the American army. South of this lake lay two others, Xochimilco and Chalco, the latter extending farther to the east. The highroad from Puebla to the City of Mexico, after rounding the northeastern corner of Lake Chalco, traversed a long and narrow isthmus between the lakes, and so at last reached open ground in front of the ancient city. It was upon

this isthmus, behind formidable fortifications on a
rocky hill known as the Peñon Viejo, that the army
of Santa Anna lay in wait. To guard against a
flanking movement by the Americans, who might
conceivably make a wide detour round Texcoco,
another army was in position northeast of the lake.

Did the failure to hold the mountain passes mean
that Santa Anna was really playing into Scott's
hand? Whatever Santa Anna's secret purpose at
that time, Scott had no delusions about his immediate intention. Santa Anna would make a genuine resistance under the eye of the capital. Grim
battle crowned by a crushing victory seemed to
Scott the imperative necessity. On the east shore
of Lake Chalco Scott paused to think. To attack
along the isthmus would be Thermopylæ over
again; he therefore promptly dismissed the idea.
The flanking movement round Texcoco did not
commend itself to him. Was there any third plan?
To the Mexican mind there apparently was not.
Santa Anna had not even now learned the lesson of
Cerro Gordo. The strip of broken country south of
Lake Chalco, where its waters approached the feet
of the mountains, seemed to him closed by nature.
To the men who had dragged their cannon by hand
through the chasms at Cerro Gordo it did not seem

impassable. Scott, who had been considering this plan all along, determined to attempt it.

Now began the strategic move that was the turning-point of the war. Scott sent a column against the Peñon to serve as a blind, while he swung the bulk of his army round through the difficult country south of the lake. The movement, in comparison with that at Cerro Gordo, proved only moderately difficult. On the 18th of August Scott established his headquarters at the village of San Agustín de las Cuevas, west of Lake Chalco, on the highroad between the City and Acapulco.

Scott had won his first move; but had he actually bettered his position? Santa Anna, perceiving what his opponent was about, had withdrawn from the isthmus, and had also established himself on the Acapulco road. Three miles north of San Agustin the great hacienda of San Antonio had been fortified by the Mexicans. Two miles farther to the north the road was again blocked by the extensive fortifications of Churubusco. And what of the road itself? Was it, like the isthmus road, a Thermopylæ? Scott's engineers reported it was much the same thing. On the east were Lake Xochimilco and its marshes; on the west, an ancient lava field, the Pedregal, fissured into a labyrinth of chasms worse than the mountains at Cerro Gordo. If Scott could not somehow continue his turning movement, his first success in strategy would be of little value.

Four miles to the west of the Acapulco road, beyond the Pedregal, there was another road, connecting the capital with the village of San Angel and continuing southward through a narrow valley past the farm of Padierna to Contreras. Could this be reached by skirting the southern edge of the Pedregal? Encouraged by the belief of his engineers that it could, Scott decided on a second turning movement toward the west. Leaving General Worth to threaten San Antonio, Scott himself started a column along the skirts of the Pedregal. It was hard work, and the men had to march light, opening a road as they went. But again the Americans proved equal to the task and forced their way past the Pedregal until they appeared before the village of Padierna on the San Angel road.[1]

Meanwhile Santa Anna, though with less confidence than in the earlier stage of the game, sought

[1] Through a confusion of names by the Americans, the fighting on the San Angel road was known at that time as the battle of Contreras.

to prepare against a further move of the Americans toward the west. The army that had guarded the north end of Lake Texcoco, commanded by General Valencia, was brought around to the west of the lake and was sent forward to hold the San Angel road. Valencia, advancing as far as Padierna, guessed what Scott was about and decided to fortify the west side of the valley in which Padierna lies. On the 18th of August Scott's advance guard encountered his outposts. After a brief skirmish the Americans withdrew. Santa Anna, fearing that the Americans might get between him and Valencia, ordered the Mexican general to fall back along the San Angel road in order to be in closer touch with the forces at Churubusco. But Valencia, who was his political rival and was eager to make a reputation, refused to obey.

At Padierna, in the afternoon of the 19th of August, Valencia was attacked. The Americans, however, did not press the attack but contented themselves with long-range firing. Realizing that Valencia's position was too strong to be taken in front, the Americans had decided upon another audacious turning movement. After an engineering reconnaissance, an infantry column under General Riley was sent out to do just what Santa

Anna had feared — to get between him and Valencia and come down on Padierna from the rear. Now the Americans did their best marching, "most difficult and tedious, passing over volcanic rocks and across large fissures barely narrow enough to permit the men to get over them by leaping." Their path was through the heart of the Pedregal. Another brigade, commanded by General Cadwalader, followed, and then another, commanded by General P. F. Smith, who took command of the whole expedition. By nightfall these forces were in part on the San Angel road some distance north of Padierna and in part beyond it at the village of San Gerónimo. Just as night fell they were menaced by a large force of Mexicans advancing down the San Angel road from the north.

Such was the hazardous situation of the armies along the San Angel road in the late afternoon, as Scott observed it from a high hill opposite Padierna. The swift approach of night induced both sides to stand where they were and wait for morning. Scott laid a new plan for the next day. He realized that to some extent — he did not as yet know how far — Santa Anna had again paralleled his western movement. This accounted for the unexpected advance of the Mexicans southward along the San

Angel road. To deal with this new turn of events a double battle would have to be fought next day — with Valencia at Padierna and with the newcomers at San Gerónimo. Reinforcements were therefore ordered to San Gerónimo over the difficult path through the Pedregal.

That night a tempest swept the Pedregal and the San Angel road. Again a difference of morale was revealed in the opposing armies. The Americans at San Gerónimo, though without cover, stood their ground in the midst of the storm. The Mexicans who had menaced them at nightfall drew back to find shelter in the villages toward the north. While the storm raged Captain Robert E. Lee performed what Scott described as "the greatest feat of moral and physical courage performed by any individual, to my knowledge, pending the campaign." Through the dark and the driving rain he contrived to make his way back from San Gerónimo, across the fissures of the Pedregal, to headquarters, where he reported that the officers at San Gerónimo advised a sudden concentration on the position of Valencia immediately before daybreak. Scott approved the plan, and Lee returned through the night to San Gerónimo.

*VIEW OF CHAPULTEPEC AND MOLINO DEL REY,
AFTER THE BATTLE OF SEPTEMBER 8, 1847*

Lithograph by N. Currier, after a sketch by H. Meendez, taken from the Casa del Mata. In the Print Department of the Library of Congress, Washington.

Lithograph by N. Currier, after a sketch by H. Mécendez, taken from the Casa del Mata. In the Print Department of the Library of Congress, Washington.

The Mexicans at Padierna seem to have vacillated between exultation and hysterics. Valencia wrote boastful dispatches dated at "the triumphal camp of Padierna"; he promoted officers; he also raved against Santa Anna whom he charged with abandoning him to the Americans. Meanwhile Smith prepared to move along the mountains at Valencia's back and take his position in the rear. It was three in the morning of Friday, the 20th of August, when the Americans — who had had no tents during the tempest and but little food — started from San Gerónimo. At six o'clock, they burst upon Valencia's camp. Just seventeen minutes were sufficient for the business. Valencia fled. His men fled. A torrent of panic-stricken Mexicans poured down into the San Angel road and along it pell-mell toward the north, pursued by the Americans. The fugitives met that other Mexican army which had weakly retreated to find shelter from the tempest while the Americans had endured their hardships and had gone forward to victory. This second army, which was really the main army commanded by Santa Anna himself, was appalled by the rout of Valencia's army and, catching the spirit of retreat, rapidly fell back toward the north.

The force under Worth that was watching San
Antonio had also found its opportunity. While
Scott pressed the pursuit along the San Angel road
he notified Worth that he would soon be able to
swing round on San Antonio from behind, and that
Worth as soon as he heard the sound of such an
attack was to move against San Antonio from the
front. Worth exceeded his instructions and pushed
his command forward earlier than Scott had intended. In the forenoon of the 20th of August the
two sections of the American army were thus moving northward on parallel lines still separated by
the wilderness of the Pedregal — Scott along the
San Angel road, Worth along the Acapulco road.

On both roads the Mexicans were retiring. Before Scott they were in full retreat. Before Worth
they began to withdraw as soon as they heard of
the disaster on the other road, which had now made
San Antonio an untenable position. Pressing after
them, Worth converted their retirement into a
rout, followed them through San Antonio, and
continued along the Acapulco road until he faced
the strong defenses of Churubusco.

About the same time Scott, driving the Mexicans
before him in like manner, had reached the village
of Coyoacán, southwest of Churubusco, where three

roads opened before him — one southeast to San Antonio, one northeast to Churubusco, one northwest to the city. It was from Coyoacán that Scott had intended to swing round and take San Antonio from behind, advancing by the first of the three roads. From the steeple of the village church, San Antonio could be seen as well as that portion of the Acapulco road between San Antonio and Churubusco. An officer sent into the belfry reported that the Mexicans were retreating from San Antonio upon Churubusco. Scott's plan of action was no longer of use. Should he now advance by the northeast road and join Worth at Churubusco or advance by the northwest road, leaving Worth to his own devices, and either turn Churubusco from the west or continue straight on to the city gates? The decision he reached has been hotly discussed both by participants in the event that followed and by later students. Perhaps it is fair to say that the bulk of opinion views Scott's next movement as a hasty blunder and holds that the success which closed this famous day was due not to generalship but to sheer hard fighting.[1]

---

[1] The opposite view is skillfully defended by the latest specialist in this field, Justin H. Smith, who holds that Scott took the only course open to him. See *The War with Mexico*, vol. II, p. 112.

Scott resolved to attack Churubusco and thus unite with Worth and get complete control of the Acapulco road. It is not denied by his friends that he was ill-informed as to the defenses of Churubusco, that he did not fully comprehend what he was undertaking. His detractors insist that he should have turned this position as already he had turned the isthmus and San Antonio; that it ought to have been regarded as too strong for a direct attack; that only the personal superiority of the American soldier to the Mexican soldier retrieved Scott's mistake and saved him from a repulse.

The Mexican position, roughly speaking, was like a fan opening from a bridge-head where the Acapulco road crossed the Churubusco River. The bridge-head itself was strongly fortified. South of the river, like the ribs of the fan, heavy masses of building had been incorporated in the defenses. Conspicuous among these was the old convent of San Mateo, which Mr. Rives describes as:

a venerable building dating from the year 1678, which still remains one of the most interesting and attractive objects in the immediate neighborhood of the City of Mexico. The little convent church, now rarely used, is of solid and somber Spanish masonry, but is finished on its western front with blue tiles, or *azulejos*, which add a delightful touch to the quaintness and incomparable charm of the group of buildings. On the south side of the church is a beautiful patio with a gallery on the second story, and orange trees blossoming in the midst of it add beauty and perfume to the secluded spot. The convent is surrounded with large gardens which must once have been cultivated by the Franciscan brothers, and about which stood, and still stands, a strong masonry wall some twelve feet in height, the whole constituting a very formidable place of defense.

In addition to the defensive advantage which this masonry offered, there were the Mexican entrenchments. Both these and the convent lay south of the river, a small stream flowing due east. North of the river large masses of Mexican infantry were posted.

In the course of the afternoon the Americans carried on simultaneously, but without much co-operation, three different attacks on this strong position. Worth, advancing from San Antonio, entered the village of Churubusco from the southeast, aiming straight at the bridge-head. General Twiggs advanced from Cayoacán on the southwest to the storming of the convent. A third column, under the command of General Franklin Pierce, — presently to be replaced by General Shields — was sent across the river, some distance to the

west, with orders to march round behind Churubusco, seize the Acapulco road north of the bridge,
and attack the Mexicans from the rear. Scott's
headquarters remained at Cayoacán, from whose
belfry Churubusco was in plain view.

The fighting which now took place proved to be
the sternest which the Americans had yet encountered. Hitherto they had been opposed chiefly
by Indian conscripts with little interest in the
war. Now a large number of their opponents
were Spanish Mexicans, who were reinforced by a
considerable number of deserters from the American army — impetuous Irishmen who had been
won over by secret agents of the Mexican Government and were now known as the "Companions of
St. Patrick." These men, likely to fight desper-
ately because they knew that capture probably
meant death, were placed in the key position at
the bridge-head.

For some time the struggle was merely a furious
fight; each of the three columns conducted its own
battle, and each attacked from a different point of
the compass. It was at their extreme left, after an
American column had crossed the river that the
Mexicans first gave way. Thereupon Worth flung all
his strength upon the bridge-head and finally carried

it with the bayonet. The Mexicans made their last stand in the convent. When they no longer had hope, a white flag from the church tower brought the engagement to a close. Churubusco had fallen.

What forces were engaged on the Mexican side in these days of their great defeat is not definitely known. The number was probably about twenty thousand, though not more than nine or ten thousand were in action at Churubusco. The Mexican losses are also largely conjecture. Nearly three thousand men were taken prisoner. Among these were a number of the American deserters, who received, after trial by court martial, the last severities of military law. As to the American forces, out of about eight thousand actually engaged the total loss, during the two days of fighting (the 19th and 20th of August), was about a thousand men.

Taken altogether, these brilliant actions — often spoken of as two, and even three, separate battles, [1] though really one expanding design to drive the Mexicans from Churubusco — shattered the outer defenses of the City of Mexico and placed a triumphant American army at its very gates.

[1] Named Contreras, San Antonio, Churubusco.

CHAPTER XIV

THE CONQUERED PEACE

THE last gunshot at Churubusco should have ended
the Mexican War. Yet it did not. There were
still, though probably without justification, three
hard fought engagements. One of these was not
only unnecessary but was also the bloodiest event
of the war — the slaughter of the Molino del Rey.
Scott's course of action in this last chapter of the
war is not explained by his own statements, especially the senseless armistice which he now concluded with Santa Anna. The theory of Scott's
enemies is that he was playing politics with his eye
on the presidency and that, in his eagerness to gain
popularity by making peace, he was trapped by
Santa Anna. According to a more generous theory Scott was still Santa Anna's dupe and really
thought that the Mexican was eager for the end
and that Churubusco had given him the excuse he
was seeking. If so, we can understand Scott's

prompt acceptance of Santa Anna's application for an armistice — decided upon, apparently, before the cannon smoke was well off the roof-tops of Churubusco.

Now followed two weeks of inaction for the Americans while Santa Anna, under cover of negotiations, stealthily reconstructed his defenses and reorganized his army. After that, Santa Anna dropped the mask, and Scott, having now to endure being placed before the world's eye as Santa Anna's dupe, resumed the offensive.[1]

The renewed operations of the Americans began with the horrible attack on the Molino del Rey, a group of massive stone buildings at the foot of the storied hill of Chapultepec. Scott, who had heard that this place was used as a cannon foundry, now ordered its destruction. After an assault which was so stubbornly resisted as to cause a grim mortality among the Americans, the mill was taken. No cannon foundry was discovered. Scott, perhaps because of chagrin at seeing how plainly Santa Anna was his master in diplomacy, had again blundered. After this costly battle the Americans

[1] Mr. Justin H. Smith, in the second volume of *The War with Mexico*, holds a brief for Scott as diplomat no less than as general. Scott's case will never be more subtly argued. But one may applaud the skill of an advocate without accepting his conclusions.

marched back to their camp. The action had been perfectly fruitless and had greatly weakened Scott's force.

His next move was the storming of Chapultepec. Here is an incident in the war which will live forever in the American imagination, for never have Americans, not even at Château-Thierry, given a better account of themselves in the deadly work of the bayonet. The steep hill of Chapultepec, crowned by an old palace of the Mexican viceroys, had been well fortified. Against the advice of his best engineers, Scott decided that its garrison must be dislodged. Again there was furious hand-to-hand fighting. The terraces of Chapultepec literally ran with blood. During the storming the American officers for a while lost control of their men, and no quarter was given. This was in revenge for a base incident in the previous battle, when, in an interval during which the Americans had fallen back under heavy fire from the walls of the Molino del Rey, the Mexicans had sallied forth and murdered the prostrate wounded. It was this bit of savagery that was repaid with interest.

Though at a frightful cost, Scott had now shattered the second line of defense before Mexico

City. Without a pause in his hammerlike blows, he crashed on into the city itself. On September 13, 1847, two American columns drove through its gates. Santa Anna with what he could rally of its garrison escaped into the suburbs and fixed his headquarters at Guadalupe Hidalgo. Early in the morning of the fourteenth the Americans were in possession of the capital of Mexico.

The loss of the city was a heavy blow, but Santa Anna was not yet ready to abandon the game. With the remnant of his troops he was planning to overwhelm the American garrison at Puebla and so cut off Scott from his base of supplies, when he was forced to resign the presidency.[1]

The office devolved upon the presiding justice of the Supreme Court, Manuel de la Peña y Peña, the same man who as Foreign Secretary had invited an ambassador from the United States and then had not dared receive him. At Querétaro, Peña y Peña succeeded in establishing a provisional government that was recognized both at home and abroad. He was still a moderate in politics, steeled to accept the accomplished fact, eager for peace.

[1] Shortly afterward Santa Anna once more sought safety in exile. As he had entered Mexico by American connivance, he abandoned it, appropriately enough, under an American safe-conduct.

Behind him among the moderates was such common sense as Mexico possessed. Opposed to him were various factions, all fantastic, ranging from monarchists to extreme republicans, some bent upon dragging out the war into an endless guerilla conflict which the United States might at last abandon, some equally opposed to peace because they believed that only through annexation to the United States could republicanism become secure in Mexico. Now for the last time that stubborn ghost of a British intervention was raised and laid. An inquiry from Mexico whether England would guarantee peace between Mexico and the United States, followed by England's positive refusal to intervene, left the new Government alone with its difficulty. Peña y Peña had hoped to work at his problem with characteristic Mexican deliberation. But shortly after Trist began negotiations, a dispatch arrived from Washington depriving him of authority and ordering him home — apparently because Polk thought he was becoming merciful toward the enemy. Peña y Peña was terrified. What might this portend? Was anything behind it except dissatisfaction with an agent who paid little attention to instructions? Trist made crafty use of the dispatch, pressing Peña y Peña to arm him with a signed treaty which he might take home with him in defiance of the President. He had the audacity to write to Washington, in substance, that he was the best judge of what ought to be done and would continue negotiations.

In spite of the impending crisis, Mexican diplomacy kept its usual intolerably slow course. There was desperate effort to mitigate Trist's three main demands: that the Rio Grande be accepted as the boundary of Mexico, that New Mexico and Upper California be ceded to the United States, and that the compensation therefor be only fifteen millions instead of the thirty millions which Mexico demanded. Trist made some concession by agreeing to assume the American claims that were the alleged cause of the war. On the whole, the Mexicans had reason to be glad they were dealing with Trist and not with his master at Washington. When Polk set out to "conquer a peace," he meant to have both Californias, Upper and Lower. Had he not feared opposition in Congress, he might have demanded still more.

In spite of Trist's generosity, which left the Mexicans a considerable part of their original domain, they continued the vain attempt to bargain. At last Trist and Scott, now on the best of terms, played their final trump. Trist named the day on which he would break off negotiations. Scott, through the British Chargé d'Affaires, let it be known to Peña y Peña that he was preparing to march on Querétaro. The British diplomat gave the Mexicans a broad hint that both Americans meant business and that the only way to stop them was to sign a satisfactory treaty. Peña y Peña yielded. In the evening of the day Trist had named, a courier from Querétaro, riding posthaste, brought to the Mexican commissioners at the capital instructions to sign the treaty in a form satisfactory to Trist. It was agreed, perhaps as a concession to Mexican pride, that the signing should not take place in the city. At Guadalupe Hidalgo, some twenty-four hours after the courier arrived, the commissioners of the two countries signed on February 2, 1848, the document which dismembered Mexico and added an empire to the United States. Except for that small portion of Arizona, purchased through James Gadsden six years afterward, the treaty established the southern boundary of the United States as it is today.

It is recorded of that French minister who ceded New France to Great Britain that he later claimed that he had foreseen how it would disrupt that Empire, breaking one strong power into two weak ones. Be that as it may, the addition of New France to the British Empire may have been fate's device for precipitating the American Revolution. If so, the addition to the Union of the enormous area ceded by Mexico forms a parallel, leading as it did to the series of crises which ended in the Civil War.

Over the whole matter of the Mexican cession lies the sinister shadow of party politics. It invaded the army, producing bitter quarrels between Scott and his generals. Indeed, it is hard to prove that he was not trying to make political capital out of the Mexican War and to prevent others from doing so. In spite of much talk about public duty, the same may be said of Polk. If he was not in deadly fear of Scott as a possible Whig candidate for President, at least he was very zealous in punishing his errors. Using the quarrels in the army as a pretext, Polk removed Scott from command. The victor of Contreras was not permitted to lead his army home. In the Roman sense, he was refused a triumph. Instead, he was summoned before a military court of inquiry on the conduct of the war — a court which accomplished nothing beyond spoiling the dramatic effect of the career of the leading general.

The early months of 1848 were filled with anxious debate upon the effect that peace would have on the country. Slavery questions, the Wilmot Proviso, were on every tongue. Generally, it was assumed that a great cession would be required of Mexico and that the only question now was how it should be divided between North and South. Against this assumption stood Daniel Webster, insisting that the United States should take no new territory but Texas — that only so could we escape a terrible division on the subject of slavery.

No scruples of this sort troubled the President. Though the treaty was less grasping than his desire, he determined to make the best of it. On the day that he decided to send the treaty to the Senate, by a strange coincidence, John Quincy Adams was struck with paralysis at his place in the House — February 21, 1848. The adjournment of both Houses that day and the next caused a delay, but on the twenty-third the treaty was communicated to the Senate. Webster strove in vain to defeat it. On the 10th of March it was ratified by 38 votes against 14. The opposing votes were evenly divided between Whigs and Democrats. Only four of them came from New England and the Middle States; the rest were scattered over the West and South. The majority, 26 Democrats and 12 Whigs, represented every section of the Union. When it came to the pinch, the lure of empire broke all party and sectional lines. The moment the acquisition was complete, however, all these lines were again restored and the quarrel over the spoil of Mexico soon solidified each of the two sections and rendered them bitterly self-conscious. It virtually reorganized the Union on the principle of duality by creating between the parties an unstable equilibrium. Thus was the stage set for a great and terrible civil war.

17

BIBLIOGRAPHICAL NOTE

THERE is no satisfactory, independent narrative of the
Texas episode. Of modern books, the *Texas* (American Commonwealths, 1903) of the late Professor G. P.
Garrison is excellent, but in some respects obsolete.
The chief living authority, Professor E. C. Barker, unfortunately has not written the book which he ought
to write. Very valuable essays by Professor Barker
are: *Stephen F. Austin and the Independence of Texas,
The Texan Declaration of Causes for Taking up Arms
Against Mexico,* and *Land Speculation as a Cause of
the Texas Revolution,* all in the *Quarterly* of the Texas
State Historical Association; *The Finances of the Texas Revolution* in the *Political Science Quarterly; President Jackson and the Texas Revolution* in the *American
Historical Review.* An illuminating essay is *Causes
and Origin of the Decree of April 6, 1830,* by Alleine
Howren, *Southwestern Historical Quarlerly,* vol. XVI,
pp. 378–422 (April, 1913). Valuable monographs by
Miss E. Z. Rather are *Recognition of the Republic of
Texas by the United States* and *De Witt's Colony,* both
published by the University of Texas. Many contemporaneous accounts such as the *Reminiscences* of
Henry Smith will be found in the *Quarterly* of the Texas State Historical Association, now the *Southwestern
Historical Quarterly.*

Among recent volumes that bear upon Texas, the most valuable to the general reader is, on the whole, George Lockhart Rives, *The United States and Mexico, 1821–1848* (2 vols., 1913). Its Texan chapters form a good outline of the entire episode. Justin H. Smith, *The Annexation of Texas* (1911), though important, bears too heavily on the hypothesis of a British conspiracy. More objective is Ephraim D. Adams, *British Interests and Activities in Texas* (1910). The invaluable *Diplomatic Correspondence of the Republic of Texas* has been published in three volumes as *Annual Reports* of the American Historical Association, (1907–08).

Of the great actors of the drama adequate lives are still to be written. This is true even of the greatest, Calhoun, though his latest biography by W. M. Meigs, *The Life of John Caldwell Calhoun*, 2 vols. (1917), is a most important accumulation of fact. J. S. Bassett, *The Life of Andrew Jackson*, 2 vols. (1911), has supplanted the earlier treatises but is by no means definitive. Of Rhett there is no biography. Carl Schurz, *Henry Clay* (American Statesmen, 2 vols., 1887), and H. C. Lodge, *Daniel Webster* (American Statesmen, 1883), are fairly good and very readable. The *Diary*, 4 vols. (1910), of President Polk is an invaluable document, as of course is the more famous *Memoirs* of John Quincy Adams. Of Austin there is great need of a good biography. The same may be said of Houston, who is clumsily treated by A. M. Williams, *Sam Houston* (1893), and delightfully, but briefly and perhaps too ardently, by Sarah Barnwell Elliott in her *Sam Houston* (1900).

The Mexican War is carefully treated in J. B.

McMaster, *History of the People of the United States*, vol. VII (1910); in the second volume of Rives, *The United States and Mexico, 1821–48*, 2 vols. (1913). For the general reader these supersede the older narratives. Both the student and the general reader will take keen interest in Justin H. Smith, *The War with Mexico*, 2 vols. (1920). Aiming to rid the story of the partisan interpretation fastened upon it by the Whig school of American historians, Mr. Smith is as artful in his silences as he is effective in his utterances. Incorporated in the graphic narrative and its voluminous notes are two special pleas — for Polk in the precipitation of the war, and for Scott in its conduct. As to military events, since Mr. Smith has had access probably to all existing documents of importance, many of which have never before been used by historians, his version may be considered authoritative. This work contains an extremely full bibliography. Several diaries and memoirs of great interest are still in manuscript. However, Grant's *Personal Memoirs*, 2 vols. (1885), have long been in print, as have Sherman's *Memoirs*, 2 vols. (1875), while recently there has been given to the public *The Life and Letters of George B. Meade*, 2 vols. (1913). A group of letters from Taylor have been printed under the title, *Letters from the Battle-fields of the Mexican War* (1908). Very delightful are the letters of Robert Anderson published as *An Artillery Officer in the Mexican War* (1911).

INDEX

A

Aberdeen, Earl of, succeeds Palmerston as British Foreign Secretary, 123; negotiates Quintuple Treaty, 123-24; and attempts at conciliation between Texas and Mexico, 127-29, 131-133, 138; and Oregon question, 132, 160-61; estimate of, 132-33 (note); and "Tappan Committee" of Anti-Slavery Convention, 136-139, 141, 142, 155; and Brougham, 143; denies intention of intervention in Texas, 148, 149; dispatch in Calhoun-Pakenham correspondence, 155-56; and Whig party, 158-59; illusions furnish clue to policy, 159-60, 164; invites France to join protest against annexation treaty, 161-62; and abolition, 162; diplomacy regarding annexation of Texas, 162-63; and Pakenham, 165, 166; decides on amicable policy toward United States, 166-67; on acquisition of California, 183

Abolition, Adams and, 94-95, 103, 104, 116-17; crisis in anti-slavery agitation, 103-104; and Texas, 104-05; *Address to the People of the Free States,*117-18;*see also* Slavery

Abolitionists, convention in London (1843), 135-39

Acapulco road, Worth on the, 242

Adams, J. Q., as a diplomat, 19, 22; Poinsett's letter to, 21; offers to buy Texan country, 22; submits Poinsett's treaties to Senate, 28; defeated by Jackson, 28; charges against Administration, 91, 180; and abolition, 94-95, 103, 104, 116-17; "Texas Speech," 108-09; and Jones's expedition, 116-117; Andrews and Tappan visit, 135-36; opinion of British motives, 140; manifesto, 145; Almonte and, 152; struck with paralysis (1848), 256

Agua Nueva, Taylor at, 203

Alaman, Lúcas, Mexican Minister of Foreign Relations, 32; *Iniciativa*, 31, 33

Alamo, Cos surrenders at the, 67; Travis's force at the, 70; massacre, 72-74; "Remember the Alamo," 86

Almonte, Colonel, and Lundy, 104; views taken by Adams, 105; Mexican Minister at Washington, 152-53, 154; demands passports, 177

Ampudia, General Pedro, at Monterey, 199

Anáhuac, port for free importation of necessities, 38;